Winslow Upton

Star Atlas

Winslow Upton

Star Atlas

ISBN/EAN: 9783337365509

Printed in Europe, USA, Canada, Australia, Japan

Cover: Foto ©Suzi / pixelio.de

More available books at **www.hansebooks.com**

STAR ATLAS

CONTAINING

STARS VISIBLE TO THE NAKED EYE

AND

CLUSTERS, NEBULÆ AND DOUBLE STARS
VISIBLE IN SMALL TELESCOPES

TOGETHER WITH

VARIABLE STARS, RED STARS, CHARACTERISTIC STAR GROUPS
ANCIENT CONSTELLATION FIGURES

AND AN

EXPLANATORY TEXT

BY

WINSLOW UPTON, A.M.
PROFESSOR OF ASTRONOMY IN BROWN UNIVERSITY

BOSTON, U.S.A., AND LONDON
GINN & COMPANY, PUBLISHERS
The Athenæum Press
1896

PREFACE.

This atlas is designed for teachers and students of Astronomy. Its aim is to supply maps for those who desire to familiarize themselves with the characteristic star groups, and also to include the leading objects of interest in the sky, which those possessing small telescopes may wish to examine. As the purpose of the atlas is educational rather than professional, it has been constructed in a form which it is hoped will be specially adapted to its use, and it contains some features and omits others which would find a place in an atlas for professional use.

The maps are on a large scale and are few in number, with liberal overlaps. Conforming with the plan of systematic study outlined in the text there are six maps, — two circumpolar, and four whose areas cover the region between declination N. 40° and S. 40.° They are subdivided into four divisions corresponding with the four divisions into which the sky is divided by the equinoctial and solstitial colures. The projection is stereographic, chosen chiefly because of the gradual narrowing of the hour circles on the equatorial maps as the declination increases, and the better correspondence of the equatorial and polar maps at their marginal overlaps. The six skeleton maps are reduced from the larger ones, and are designed to give the characteristic stellar figures of each constellation area with greater prominence than they appear on the larger maps. This is secured by omitting the fainter stars and the historical figures, and by connecting the stars by guiding lines.

The educational purpose of the atlas has caused the retention of the outlines of the historical figures, which are usually omitted on professional atlases. They are given in merest outline and for the older constellations of the northern sky only, because of frequent allusions to them in literature. Similar figures were supplied by those astronomers of the eighteenth and nineteenth centuries who completed the system of constellations in the southern hemisphere, but they were added when the use of the figures was becoming obsolete; they are of decidedly inferior character in their subjects, since they include such mechanical objects as air-pump, clock, telescope, chemical furnace; and they have no place in literature. For these reasons they are not reproduced.

The purpose of the atlas required its preparation according to the best astronomical authorities of to-day. The prevailing usage of modern astronomers has been the criterion adopted; where usage varies, a decision was necessary, and it has been made with great care. The only place where any serious difficulty has arisen has been the proper location of the boundaries between the constellation areas, in which there is no general agreement.

The epoch of the atlas is 1900, and the star places have all been reduced from various catalogues to that epoch before charting.

The stars charted are those down to the 6.0 magnitude, thus including those readily visible to the naked eye. A large number of faint stars rarely visible without a telescope, and which crowd an atlas, were thus omitted. The authority for the magnitudes is Harvard Photometry, and its extension to the south pole, vols. xiv, xxiv, and xxxiv of the Annals of the Astronomical Observatory of Harvard College.

Argelander's Uranometria Nova is the basis of the boundaries between the constellation areas, and also of the outlines of the historical figures. Behrmann's extension of the constellations to the southern pole on Argelander's plan has been adopted on the large maps, and Gould's revision, which supersedes Argelander's south of 10° N. declination, for the smaller maps.

The designations of the stars follow Argelander, Behrmann, Heis, and Gould. The added letters of Gould are used except where his revision of the areas places a star in another constellation.

The Milky Way is drawn only approximately, based upon the drawings of Heis and Gould.

The meanings of the Arabic names of stars are taken from Higgins' Arabic Names of Stars.

The clusters and nebulæ charted were selected from Dreyer's New Catalogue, the variables from Chandler's Second Catalogue, the colored stars from the list in Chambers' Astronomy and from the notes in Gould's Uranometria Argentina and other catalogues. The double stars include those within the limits adopted which are catalogued in Webb's Celestial Objects, and those mentioned by Gould and others. The authority for the positions and notes in the table is Crossley, Gledhill, and Wilson's Handbook of Double Stars, and more recent publications of various observers.

The work has been done independently of other publications, but comparisons have been made with other atlases and star lists in order to secure freedom from error as far as possible.

Acknowledgment for advice is due and is gratefully made to several astronomers and educators who have been consulted, especially to Prof. E. C. Pickering, Prof. C. A. Young, and Mr. D. W. Hoyt. The reproduction of the outlines of the historical figures is due to the skill of Mr. N. M. Isham of Brown University and the engravers Messrs. Bradley and Poates.

WINSLOW UPTON.

BROWN UNIVERSITY, PROVIDENCE, R. I.,
June, 1896.

EXPLANATORY TEXT.

THE CONSTELLATIONS.

THE division of the sky into constellations is the oldest part of the science of Astronomy. It was begun in prehistoric times by Chaldean and Egyptian astronomers, and was further developed by the Greeks. The Arabian scholars of the Middle Ages received the system from the Greeks and handed it down, with a few modifications, to European astronomers. Many additions and alterations were made by astronomers after the sixteenth century. To-day the system is still used, but only for purposes of notation, and it has ceased to be of much importance in the strict science of Astronomy.

The primitive astronomers adopted the pictorial plan of distinguishing the stars.

ived
iong
ions.
, our
iefly
tury
the
stel-
fied,
that
but
udy.
was
i the
l list

the
> us,

ERRATA.

PAGE 27. Third sentence from foot should read: *Cassiopeia* is above the pole towards the right, *Ursa Major* low in the sky below the pole.

MAPS I AND VI. The names of the months should be changed from January to July, from February to August, and so on.

but in Ptolemy's and in subsequent star catalogues the position of each star is given in two ways : (1) by its place in the constellation figure, and (2) by the system of longitude and latitude which the Greeks had adopted. The latter system enables the modern astronomer to identify the stars, and the former to reproduce the outline of the figure with partial success, depending upon the character of the figure and upon the number of the stars in the group. Where the constellation has but few stars, as *Canis Minor*, which has but two stars in Ptolemy's catalogue, the reproduction of the traditional figure is very uncertain. In the sixteenth century, the German astronomer Heinfogel secured the assistance of the artist Albrecht Dürer in reproducing the classic figures, and his highly embellished drawings formed the basis of the figures given on globes and atlases until the nineteenth century.[2] Present atlases either omit them entirely, or give them in merest outline because of their historical interest and the frequent allusions to them in literature. They have ceased to have any use in modern Astronomy.

The first change in the system of constellations described by Ptolemy was made by transferring the name of the constellation from the space included within the outlines of

[1] Baily's edition in Memoirs R. A. S., vol. xiii.   [2] Annales Astronomiques, I, 1878.

telescope, and which crowd an atlas, were thus omitted. The authority for the magnitudes is Harvard Photometry, and its extension to the south pole, vols. xiv, xxiv, and xxxiv of the Annals of the Astronomical Observatory of Harvard College.

Argelander's Uranometria Nova is the basis of the boundaries between the constellation areas, and also of the outlines of the historical figures. Behrmann's extension of the constellations to the southern pole on Argelander's plan has been adopted on the large maps, and Gould's revision, which supersedes Argelander's south of 10° N. declination, for the smaller maps.

The designations of the stars follow Argelander, Behrmann, Heis, and Gould. The added letters of Gould are used except where his revision of the areas places a star in another constellation.

The Milky Way is drawn only approximately, based upon the drawings of Heis and Gould.

Th

of Star

Th

variable

Astrono

The dot

Celestia

tions a1

and me

Th

been m

as poss

A

educate

and M1

the ski...

Poates.

WINSLOW UPTON.

BROWN UNIVERSITY, PROVIDENCE, R. I.,
June, 1896.

EXPLANATORY TEXT.

THE CONSTELLATIONS.

THE division of the sky into constellations is the oldest part of the science of Astronomy. It was begun in prehistoric times by Chaldean and Egyptian astronomers, and was further developed by the Greeks. The Arabian scholars of the Middle Ages received the system from the Greeks and handed it down, with a few modifications, to European astronomers. Many additions and alterations were made by astronomers after the sixteenth century. To-day the system is still used, but only for purposes of notation, and it has ceased to be of much importance in the strict science of Astronomy.

The primitive astronomers adopted the pictorial plan of distinguishing the stars. They selected from the heavens prominent groups of stars, gave to them names derived from natural objects or from their mythology, and imagined figures to be drawn among the stars to represent the objects. Thus was formed the ancient system of constellations. Many of them are mentioned by early writers such as Homer, Hesiod, and Aratus, but our knowledge of the definite location of the groups to which they allude is derived chiefly from the star catalogue of the Greek astronomer Ptolemy, who lived in the second century of the Christian era. This star catalogue [1] contains 1028 stars and is made up of the brighter stars visible in northern latitudes. It groups the stars into forty-eight constellations, which include 926 of the whole number; the others are mentioned as unclassified, and are given as additional to the constellations near which they lie. It is probable that the early astronomers did not intend to map out the whole sky into constellations, but simply to select the prominent groups and give them names for convenience in their study. Astrology furnished the motive for the classification, and the study of the star groups was directed to the determination, if possible, of the influence which the groups had upon the earth and its inhabitants. Some prominent stars, as *Arcturus*, were in the unclassified list and not in any constellation.

The individual stars were named from their positions in the figures which the astronomers drew among the stars. The figures themselves have not come down to us, but in Ptolemy's and in subsequent star catalogues the position of each star is given in two ways: (1) by its place in the constellation figure, and (2) by the system of longitude and latitude which the Greeks had adopted. The latter system enables the modern astronomer to identify the stars, and the former to reproduce the outline of the figure with partial success, depending upon the character of the figure and upon the number of the stars in the group. Where the constellation has but few stars, as *Canis Minor*, which has but two stars in Ptolemy's catalogue, the reproduction of the traditional figure is very uncertain. In the sixteenth century, the German astronomer Heinfogel secured the assistance of the artist Albrecht Dürer in reproducing the classic figures, and his highly embellished drawings formed the basis of the figures given on globes and atlases until the nineteenth century. [2] Present atlases either omit them entirely, or give them in merest outline because of their historical interest and the frequent allusions to them in literature. They have ceased to have any use in modern Astronomy.

The first change in the system of constellations described by Ptolemy was made by transferring the name of the constellation from the space included within the outlines of

[1] Baily's edition in Memoirs R. A. S., vol. xiii.   [2] Annales Astronomiques, I, 1878.

the figure to a larger space in the sky, within which the figure represented by the name was included. Then new constellations were added in the spaces between the original groups, with the design of covering the whole sky with constellations. The new constellations were added chiefly by astronomers between the sixteenth and nineteenth centuries, who worked independently of each other. As a result there was no agreement either in the new constellations or in the drawing of the boundaries between adjacent areas. To-day there is still disagreement on both these points; professional astronomers use different designations for different parts of the sky, and star atlases are not in harmony with each other, especially for the constellations in the southern hemisphere.

The ancient system of the constellations, with its subsequent additions, survives in modern Astronomy simply as a means of subdividing the heavens and of giving names to the areas thus set apart. As the system has been one of growth, without any distinct plan except the separation of prominent groups of stars, the resulting areas are of various sizes and shapes. In a few cases the constellation figures crossed each other; the best example of this is the constellation *Serpens*, which crossed *Ophiuchus*, the figure representing the serpent-carrier holding the serpent in his hands. In the modern atlas the area called *Serpens* is divided into two portions, the western part, marked *Caput*, and the eastern, *Cauda*, to correspond with the positions of the head and the tail of the serpent, and the area named *Ophiuchus* extends between them. In some cases, moreover, the same star was in more than one figure. Thus the northeastern star in the " Square of Pegasus " is given in Bayer's Atlas both as δ *Pegasi* and also as α *Andromedæ*.

Not only are the constellation areas of various sizes, but there is no law by which the boundaries between them can be definitely marked. The aim of the compilers of atlases has been to preserve the relation of the areas to the ancient figures as far as possible. The lack of concerted action has necessarily resulted in variety of treatment, and the matter of the position of the boundaries is of such minor importance in modern Astronomy that little interest has been shown in the various schemes proposed for rectifying the boundaries. A radical change was suggested by Sir John Herschel in 1841 [1]; he advocated a complete rearrangement of the areas, especially of those in the southern sky, and proposed that each area be made a quadrilateral bounded by arcs of hour circles and parallels of declinations. This scheme did not meet with favor, but it was revived in a modified form by Dr. Gould in 1879,[2] for the southern constellations, and their boundaries were drawn by arcs of hour circles or of other great circles and parallels of declination. The new system of boundaries was made to depart from the former system at the parallel 10° north declination, and all the areas south of this region were bounded by definite arcs on the above plan instead of by the irregular lines formerly represented. This system is coming into extensive use, as it is employed for the designation of variable stars, — the only growing branch of modern Astronomy in which new star names are needed. The old areas are, however, still retained by some astronomers in preference to the revised areas, and stars previously named on the old plan, which under the new plan would require renaming, are usually mentioned under their earlier names.

In this star atlas the constellation areas are named and their boundaries are defined according to modern usage; where usage varies it has been necessary to adopt one in preference to others. The Uranometry of Argelander, published in 1840, extending from the north pole to 20° or 30° south declination, has been used within these limits; and its extension to the south pole, executed on the same plan by Behrmann in 1874, has been used for the remainder of the sky. On the smaller maps containing the characteristic star

---

[1] Memoirs R. A. S., vol. xii.   [2] Uranometria Argentina.

groups of the constellation areas, the boundaries adopted have been those of Argelander from the north pole to 10° north declination, and the reformed boundaries of Gould from that parallel southward.

NAMES OF THE CONSTELLATIONS.

The following table contains the names of the constellations included in this atlas. They are given in their Latin form, which is almost universally used, with accents to assist in their pronunciation. The genitive case of the name is also appended, as it is used in the designations of the brighter stars in each constellation. Other columns contain the meaning of each word, where it is not a proper name, and the map or maps upon which it is found. The name of the proposer of the constellation is appended. The letter P in this column indicates that the constellation was in Ptolemy's catalogue, and therefore belongs to the list of constellations used by the ancient astronomers. The twelve constellations ascribed to Bayer were introduced into his atlas from earlier observations. The origin of *Crux* and *Columba* is not definitely known, and some of Hevelius' constellations were in use before his time. The constellation *Argo* is usually subdivided into four parts, named *Carina*, *Malus*, *Puppis*, and *Vela*. The genitive *Argus* is often used with stars designated by Greek letters, but the modern tendency is to use the genitive of the name of the subdivision in which each star is situated.

TABLE I. — THE CONSTELLATIONS.

No.	Name.	Genitive.	Meaning.	Map.	Proposer.
1	Androm'-eda	Androm'-edæ		I, II	P
2	Ant'-lia	Ant'-liæ	Air pump	III	Lacaille
3	A'-pus	Ap'-odis	Bird of Paradise	VI	Bayer
4	Aqua'-rius	Aqua'-rii	Water carrier	V	P
5	A'-quila	A'-quilæ	Eagle	V	P
6	A'-ra	A'-ræ	Altar	VI	P
..	Ar'-go (Navis)	Ar'-gus	Ship Argo	III, VI	P
7	A'-ries	Ari'-etis	Ram	II	P
8	Auri'-ga	Auri'-gæ	Charioteer	I, II, III	P
9	Boo'-tes	Boo'-tis	Bear keeper	I, IV	P
10	Cæ'-lum	Cæ'-li	Sculptor's chisel	II, VI	Lacaille
11	Camelopar'-dalis	Camelopar'-dalis	Giraffe	I	Hevelius
12	Can'-cer	Can'-cri	Crab	III	P
13	Ca'-nes Venat'-ici	Ca'-num Venatico'-rum	Hunting dogs	I, IV	Hevelius
14	Ca'-nis Ma'-jor	Ca'-nis Majo'-ris	Greater dog	III	P
15	Ca'-nis Mi'-nor	Ca'-nis Mino'-ris	Lesser dog	III	P
16	Capricor'-nus	Capricor'-ni	Goat	V	P
17	Cari'-na	Cari'-næ	Keel (of ship Argo)	VI	—
18	Cassiope'-ia	Cassiope'-iæ		I	P
19	Centau'-rus	Centau'-ri	Centaur	IV, VI	P
20	Ce'-pheus	Ce'-phei		I	P
21	Ce'-tus	Ce'-ti	Whale	II	P
22	Chamæ'-leon	Chamæleon'-tis	Chameleon	VI	Bayer
23	Cir'-cinus	Cir'-cini	Pair of compasses	VI	Lacaille
24	Colum'-ba	Colum'-bæ	Dove	II, VI	
25	Co'-ma Bereni'-ces	Co'-mæ Bereni'-ces	Berenice's hair	IV	Tycho Brahe
26	Coro'-na Austra'-lis	Coro'-næ Austra'-lis	Southern crown	V, VI	P
27	Coro'-na Borea'-lis	Coro'-næ Borea'-lis	Northern crown	IV	P
28	Cor'-vus	Cor'-vi	Crow	IV	P
29	Cra'-ter	Crate'-ris	Cup	III	P
30	Crux	Cru'-cis	Cross	VI	—
31	Cyg'-nus	Cyg'-ni	Swan	I, V	P
32	Delphi'-nus	Delphi'-ni	Dolphin	V	P

No.	Name.	Genitive.	Meaning.	Map.	Proposer.
33	Dora'-do	Dora'-dus	Sword fish	VI	Bayer
34	Dra'-co	Draco'-nis	Dragon	I	P
35	Equu'-leus	Equu'-lei	Little horse	V	P
36	Erid'-anus	Erid'-ani	River Po	II, VI	P
37	For'-nax (chemica)	Forna'-cis	Furnace	II	Lacaille
38	Gem'-ini	Gemino'-rum	Twins	III	P
39	Grus	Gru'-is	Crane	V, VI	Bayer
40	Her'-cules	Her'-culis		I, IV	P
41	Horolo'-gium	Horolo'-gii	Clock	II, VI	Lacaille
42	Hy'-dra	Hy'-dræ	Snake	III, IV	P
43	Hy'-drus	Hy'-dri	Watersnake	VI	Bayer
44	In'-dus	In'-di	Indian	VI	Bayer
45	Lacer'-ta	Lacer'-tæ	Lizard	I, V	Hevelius
46	Le'-o	Leo'-nis	Lion	III	P
47	Le'-o Mi'-nor	Leo'-nis Mino'-ris	Lesser lion	III	Hevelius
48	Le'-pus	Lep'-oris	Hare	II	P
49	Li'-bra	Li'-bræ	Balance	IV	P
50	Lu'-pus	Lu'-pi	Wolf	IV, VI	P
51	Lynx	Lyn'-cis	Lynx	I, III	Hevelius
52	Ly'-ra	Ly'-ræ	Harp	I, V	P
53	Ma'-lus	Ma'-li	Mast(of ship Argo)	III	—
54	Men'-sa (Mons Mensæ)	Men'-sæ	Table (mountain)	VI	Lacaille
55	Microsco'-pium	Microsco'-pii	Microscope	V	Lacaille
56	Monoc'-eros	Monocero'-tis	Unicorn	III	Hevelius
57	Mus'-ca	Mus'-cæ	Fly	VI	Bayer
58	Nor'-ma	Nor'-mæ	Rule	IV, VI	Lacaille
59	Oc'-tans	Octan'-tis	Octant	VI	Lacaille
60	Ophiu'-chus	Ophiu'-chi	Serpent carrier	IV, V	P
61	Ori'-on	Orio'-nis		II, III	P
62	Pa'-vo	Pavo'-nis	Peacock	VI	Bayer
63	Peg'-asus	Peg'-asi	Winged horse	V	P
64	Per'-seus	Per'-sei		I, II	P
65	Phœ'-nix	Phœni'-cis	Phœnix	II, VI	Bayer
66	Pic'-tor (Equuleus Pic-toris)	Picto'-ris	Painter's easel	VI	Lacaille
67	Pis'-ces	Pis'-cium	Fishes	II, V	P
68	Pis'-cis Austra'-lis	Pis'-cis Austra'-lis	Southern fish	V	P
69	Pup'-pis	Pup'-pis	Stern(of ship Argo)	III, VI	—
70	Retic'-ulum	Retic'-uli	Net	VI	Lacaille
71	Sagit'-ta	Sagit'-tæ	Arrow	V	P
72	Sagitta'-rius	Sagitta'-rii	Archer	V, VI	P
73	Scor'-pius	Scor'-pii	Scorpion	IV, VI	P
74	Sculp'-tor (Apparatus Sculptoris)	Sculpto'-ris	Sculptor's apparatus	II, V, VI	Lacaille
75	Scu'-tum (Sobiesii)	Scu'-ti	Shield of Sobieski	V	Hevelius
76	Ser'-pens	Serpen'-tis	Serpent	IV, V	P
77	Sex'-tans	Sextan'-tis	Sextant	III	Hevelius
78	Tau'-rus	Tau'-ri	Bull	II	P
79	Telesco'-pium	Telesco'-pii	Telescope	VI	Lacaille
80	Trian'-gulum	Trian'-guli	Triangle	II	P
81	Trian'-gulum Austra'-le	Trian'-guli Austra'-lis	Southern triangle	VI	Bayer
82	Tuca'-na	Tuca'-næ	American goose	VI	Bayer
83	Ur'-sa Ma'-jor	Ursæ Majo'-ris	Greater bear	I, III	P
84	Ur'-sa Mi'-nor	Ursæ Mino'-ris	Lesser bear	I	P
85	Ve'-la	Velo'-rum	Sails(of ship Argo)	III, VI	—
86	Vir'-go	Vir'-ginis	Virgin	IV	P
87	Vo'-lans (Piscis volans)	Volan'-tis	Flying fish	VI	Bayer
88	Vulpec'-ula (cum an-sere)	Vulpec'-ulæ	Fox with goose	V	Hevelius

The above list of constellations includes all which are generally accepted at the present time. The total number is eighty-five if *Argo* is considered as one constellation, or eighty-eight if each of its subdivisions is reckoned as a separate constellation. There are many other constellations which have been proposed by eminent astronomers and used to a limited extent.[1] Thus Bode added nine constellations, one of which, *Machina Electrica*, was inserted by Argelander in his supplementary map of the southern heavens. Lacaille substituted for *Malus* the name *Pyxis* (genitive *Pyx-idos*) mariner's compass, and this is extensively used to-day. The constellation *Antinous*, ascribed to Tycho Brahe, is included in *Aquila*; *Taurus Poniatowskii*, ascribed to Poczobut, is included in *Ophiuchus* and *Serpens*. The constellation *Libra*, which is the only one of the twelve zodiacal groups not bearing the name of an animal as the derivation of the word zodiac implies, is in Ptolemy's catalogue called *Claws* (of the Scorpion). *Scutum* is sometimes called by its Greek equivalent *Clypeus*.

DESIGNATIONS OF STARS.

Individual stars have been designated by astronomers in several different ways:

1. By their position in the constellation figure. This method is now entirely obsolete.

2. By individual names. The names have come down to us chiefly from classical and mediæval times, and are either of Latin form or in a corrupted form of the Arabic designation of the star in its constellation figure. Very few of the names are now used. The method is nearly obsolete, surviving in only a few of the brightest stars.

3. By Greek or Roman letters, followed by the name of the constellation in the genitive case of its Latin form. This method was introduced by Bayer early in the seventeenth century, who lettered the leading stars in each constellation of the northern heavens, using the Greek alphabet, and if the number of stars in the constellation exceeded the number of Greek letters, using Roman letters. The stars were lettered in the order of their brightness as far as the several magnitudes were concerned, but no attempt seems to have been made to distinguish between the stars of any given magnitude. Later astronomers have adopted the same system in constellations not in Bayer's list. Nearly all of the stars readily visible to the naked eye are designated by letters on this plan, and astronomers prefer this system to any of the others.

4. By Arabic numbers, followed by the name of the constellation in the genitive case of its Latin form. This method was introduced by Flamsteed in the seventeenth century, whose numbers follow the order of the stars in right ascension. Other astronomers used the same plan. This method is used by astronomers for stars not already lettered on Bayer's plan. Where both letters and numbers have been given, the letters are preferred.

5. By the current number in any well-known modern star catalogue. This method is used when the star has neither letter nor number.

6. By the position of the star in the sky, the system corresponding to longitude and latitude on the earth. On the celestial sphere, right ascension and declination are the terms employed. This method is used for uncatalogued stars.

The brightest stars have designations in all six of the above ways. Thus the bright star which is near the northern celestial pole was designated (1) the star at the end of the tail of the lesser bear, (2) *Gjedi, Polaris, Cynosura, Alruccabah*, (3) a *Ursæ Minoris*, (4) *1 Ursæ Minoris*. It might also be referred to under (5) as B. A. C. 360, the current number

[1] See Chambers' Astronomy, vol. iii. chap. vii, ed. 1890, and Burritt's Geography of the Heavens.

in the British Association Catalogue (or by a similar designation in any other catalogue in which it occurs), and under (6) as in right ascension 1 h. 24 min., declination + 88° 46′. Of these names, α Ursæ Minoris is preferred, but Polaris is still in frequent use; all the other designations are obsolete.

The majority of stars readily visible to the naked eye are therefore usually designated by letter and name of constellation area; a large number, especially of the fainter ones, are called by a number with the name of the constellation area; a few have individual names. The faintest stars visible without a telescope, and all requiring its aid, are referred to by their numbers in star catalogues, or by their right ascensions and declinations.

In this atlas, following present usage, the individual stars are designated by a letter or by a number, if such letter or number is in use. The individual names of stars of the first magnitude, and of a few others which are extensively used, are also given upon the maps. In referring to the stars, the letter or number should be used with the genitive of the name of the constellation given in Table I, as α Herculis, 61 Cygni. The Greek alphabet is here given.

GREEK ALPHABET.

α	alpha	ν	nu
β	beta	ξ	xi
γ	gamma	ο	om'-icron
δ	delta	π	pi
ε	eps'-ilon	ρ	rho
ζ	zeta	σ	sigma
η	eta	τ	tau
θ	theta	υ	u'-psilon
ι	iota	φ	phi
κ	kappa	χ	chi
λ	lambda	ψ	psi
μ	mu	ω	o'-mega

INDIVIDUAL STAR NAMES.

Individual names have been given to several hundred of the stars. Some were assigned by the Chaldean astronomers,[1] but the earliest which are still used date from classic times and are given in their Latin form. The Arabian astronomers added many others, the name usually describing the position of the star in the constellation figure. Individual names of the stars are now rarely employed; only those of the brightest stars survive, and even for them the designation by letters is usually preferred. In this atlas, the individual names of stars of the first magnitude are given, with a few others, as Algol, which are in general use. The following table contains names which are sometimes used, together with the preferred designation by letter with the name of the constellation, and also the meaning of the word. The pronunciation of the words derived from the Arabic is a matter of uncertainty because they appear in a corrupted form; the spelling itself is often variously given. Thus, Betelgeuse is variously written Betelgueuse, Beteigeuze, Betelgeux, Betelgeuze, and is corrupted from ibt al Jauza.[2] Its pronunciation is a matter of personal preference.

[1] Epping, Astronomisches aus Babylon.
[2] Higgins, Arabic Names of the Stars.

TABLE II. — INDIVIDUAL STAR NAMES.

Name.	Other Designation.	Meaning.
Achernar	α Eridani	The end of the river
Alcor	g Ursæ Majoris	The near one
Aldebaran	α Tauri	The eye of the bull
Alderamin	α Cephei	The arm
Alfard	α Hydræ	The solitary
Algenib	γ Pegasi	The side
Algol	β Persei	The monster
Alcaid	η Ursæ Majoris	The chief
Alioth	ε Ursæ Majoris	The tail-sheep
Almach	γ Andromedæ	The bound one
Alphecca	α Corona Borealis	The broken dish
Alpheratz	α Andromedæ	The horse
Alruccabah	α Ursæ Minoris	The chariot
Altair	α Aquilæ	The bird
Antares	α Scorpii	Equal to Mars (red color)
Arcturus	α Bootis	Guardian of the bear
Arided	α Cygni	The tail piece
Bellatrix	γ Orionis	Female warrior
Betelgeuse	α Orionis	Armpit of the giant
Canopus	α Argus	(Proper name — Menelaus' pilot)
Capella	α Aurigæ	A little she-goat
Caph	β Cassiopeiæ	Palm of the hand
Castor	α Geminorum	(Proper name)
Cynosura	α Ursæ Minoris	Dog's tail
Deneb kaitos	β Ceti	Tail of the whale
Denebola	β Leonis	Tail of the lion
Dubhe	α Ursæ Majoris	She-bear
Fomalhaut	α Piscis Australis	Mouth of the fish
Hyades	Group in Taurus	*From Greek* — to rain
Kochab	β Ursæ Minoris	Star
Markab	α Pegasi	Saddle
Megrez	δ Ursæ Majoris	Rump
Menkar	α Ceti	Nostril
Merak	β Ursæ Majoris	Flank
Mira	ο Ceti	Wonderful
Mirach	β Andromedæ	Loins
Mirfak	α Persei	Elbow
Mizar	ζ Ursæ Majoris	A girdle
Pheccla	γ Ursæ Majoris	Thigh
Pleiades		*From Greek* — to sail
Alcyone	η Tauri	⎫
Asterope	21, 22 Tauri	⎪
Atlas	27 Tauri	⎪
Celieno	g Tauri	Atlas, the nymph Pleione,
Electra	17 Tauri	and their seven
Maia	20 Tauri	daughters
Merope	23 Tauri	⎪
Pleione	28 Tauri	⎪
Taygeta	19 Tauri	⎭
Polaris	α Ursæ Minoris	Pole star
Pollux	β Geminorum	(Proper name)
Præsepe	Cluster in Cancer	Crib or manger
Procyon	α Canis Minoris	Precursor dog
Ras-Alhague	α Ophiuchi	Head of the serpent charmer
Ras-Algethi	α Herculis	Head of the kneeler
Regulus	α Leonis	Chief
Rigel	β Orionis	Foot
Scheat	β Pegasi	Foreleg
Schedar	α Cassiopeiæ	Breast
Sirius	α Canis Majoris	*From Siris* — the Nile
Spica	α Virginis	An ear of wheat
Thuban	α Draconis	A dragon
Vega	α Lyræ	Falling (eagle)

BRIGHTNESS OF THE STARS.

In Ptolemy's catalogue the stars were divided into six classes, according to their brightness. The word "magnitude" was used as the equivalent of brightness, and the first six letters of the Greek alphabet were employed in their order to distinguish the several classes. The word "magnitude" is still used in this erroneous sense, though the brightness of a star, as we see it, depends upon its distance and intrinsic light-power as well as upon its size. Stars visible to the naked eye are still subdivided into six "magnitudes," and the fainter stars revealed by the telescope are similarly grouped into those of the seventh magnitude, eighth magnitude, etc., by an extension of the same principle.

This rough classification has been made the basis of the more accurate classification which modern astronomy requires. It was found that the several orders of magnitude estimated by various astronomers differed by a light ratio very nearly $2\frac{1}{2}$. That is, a star of the third magnitude gives $2\frac{1}{2}$ times as much light as one of the fourth magnitude; one of the fourth $2\frac{1}{2}$ times as much light as one of the fifth magnitude, and so on. Modern photometric researches are made upon the assumption of this constant light ratio (the adopted ratio is 2.512 or $\sqrt[5]{100}$). In this way the modern treatment of the subject of the brightness of the stars is simply a refinement in method, but with no change of plan from that followed by the earlier astronomers and their successors. Since the stars are of every degree of brightness, the gradations are expressed upon a numerical scale, with fractions of a magnitude expressed decimally. Thus, 61 *Cygni*, which is near the dividing line between a star of the fifth and one of the sixth magnitude, is now given as of the 5.6 magnitude.

The modern system of designating the brightness of stars is, then, to express it numerically, upon a scale agreeing in general with the "magnitudes" of the earlier astronomers. First magnitude stars are those between 0.5 and 1.5 on the photometric scale, second magnitude stars are those between 1.5 and 2.5, third magnitude stars those between 2.5 and 3.5, and so on. The only important departure from the earlier system is in the case of the twenty brightest stars of the sky. The ancients included in the group of stars which they called those of the first magnitude all the brightest stars, ranging from α *Canis Majoris*, or *Sirius*, to α *Leonis*, or *Regulus*. But the former is thirteen times as bright as the latter, and therefore should be in a class nearly three magnitudes brighter. The first magnitude stars, though few in number, really belong in several classes. The actual measurement of the amount of light given by the twenty brightest stars shows that eleven of them are between 0.5 and 1.5 magnitude, and hence of the first magnitude; that seven should be placed in the next brighter division, and hence are of the zero magnitude, and that two belong in a class still brighter. As the scale has run out, the brightness of these two stars is expressed with a minus sign before it. The following table contains the list of stars generally known as first magnitude stars, rearranged according to the modern scale.[1]

---

[1] Annals Observatory of Harvard College, vol. xviii, no. 1.

TABLE III. — STARS OF THE FIRST MAGNITUDE, REARRANGED.

A. STARS BRIGHTER THAN 0 MAGNITUDE.			*C.* STARS OF 1ˢᵗ MAGNITUDE.		
NAME.	MAGNITUDE.	MAP.	NAME.	MAGNITUDE.	MAP.
α Canis Majoris (*Sirius*)	− 1.4	II, III	α Tauri (*Aldebaran*)	1.0	II
α Argûs (*Canopus*)	− 0.8	VI	α Orionis (*Betelgeuse*)	0.9	II, III
B. STARS OF 0 MAGNITUDE.			β Geminorum (*Pollux*)	1.2	III
			α Leonis (*Regulus*)	1.3	III
α Eridani (*Achernar*)	0.4	VI	α Crucis	1.0	VI
α Aurigæ (*Capella*)	0.1	I	α Virginis (*Spica*)	1.1	IV
β Orionis (*Rigel*)	0.3	II	β Centauri	0.7	VI
α Canis Minoris (*Procyon*)	0.5	III	α Scorpii (*Antares*)	1.2	IV
α Boötis (*Arcturus*)	0.2	IV	α Aquilæ (*Altair*)	0.9	V
α Centauri	0.2	VI	α Cygni (*Deneb or Arided*)	1.4	I
α Lyræ (*Vega*)	0.2	IV, V	α Piscis Australis (*Fomalhaut*)	1.3	V

STAR SYMBOLS.

In this star atlas, symbols agreeing with those used by Argelander and others have been adopted to express the several magnitudes. Stars are charted down to the 6.0 magnitude, which includes all readily visible to the naked eye. The largest symbol is used for the nine stars which are brighter than the first magnitude, the next for those of the first magnitude, that is, 0.5 to 1.5 on the photometric scale, the next symbol for those of the second magnitude, that is, 1.5 to 2.5 on the photometric scale, and so on. In the smaller maps the magnitudes are expressed by circles of progressive sizes, as there stated.

STAR CLUSTERS AND NEBULÆ.

In this atlas are indicated the star clusters and nebulæ which can be seen in small telescopes. It is not always possible to distinguish between nebulous-appearing objects which may be true nebulæ, that is, of gaseous constitution, and those which are clusters of separate stars. Sometimes, too, the same object is a cluster and nebula combined. The atlas has two different symbols, but there is sometimes doubt as to which should be employed.

The study of nebulæ requires, except in a few instances, telescopes whose apertures are at least twelve inches; in smaller instruments they appear simply as faint patches of light.

The following tables contain the principal clusters and nebulæ which are charted on the maps, their right ascensions, declinations, and the maps on which they may be found. Condensed descriptions, usually following those in Dreyer's Catalogue of Nebulæ and Clusters [1] are appended. To the list of nebulæ are also appended a few notes regarding the most important ones. The numbers in the first column are those in Dreyer's Catalogue, the letters N. G. C. standing for New General Catalogue.

[1] Memoirs R. A. S., vol. xlix.

TABLE IV. — STAR CLUSTERS.

No. N. G. C.	Right Ascension	Declination	Map	Description
104	0 h 20 m	−72° 38′	VI	very bright, very large, globular
129	0 24	59 40	I	very large, stars 9th to 13th magnitude
188	0 35	84 47	I	very large, 150–200 stars
225	0 37	61 15	I	large, stars 9th to 10th magnitude
288	0 48	−27 8	II, V	bright, large, globular
362	0 59	−71 23	VI	very bright, very large, globular
663	1 39	60 44	I	bright, large
752	1 52	37 11	II	exceedingly large, visible to eye as nebulous star
869	2 12	56 41	I	exceedingly large, stars 7th to 14th magnitude
884	2 15	56 39	I	very large, very many stars
1039	2 36	42 21	I, II	bright, very large
1245	3 8	46 52	I, II	quite large, rich in faint stars
1291	3 14	−41 28	II, VI	very bright, quite large, globular
1387	3 33	−35 51	II	very bright, quite large, globular
1399	3 35	−35 47	II	very bright, quite large, globular, easily revolved
1436	3 40	−36 26	II	very bright, globular
1528	4 8	50 59	I	bright, many stars
1787	5 0	−65 59	VI	very large, many stars
1850	5 9	−68 53	VI	very bright, large, globular, easily resolved
1851	5 11	−40 9	II, VI	very bright, very large, globular, easily resolved
1855	5 10	−68 58	VI	very bright, large
1857	5 13	39 14	II	somewhat compressed
1904	5 20	−24 37	II, III	quite large, very many stars, globular, easily resolved
1912	5 22	35 45	II, III	bright, very large, very many stars
1960	5 29	34 5	II, III	bright, very large, very many stars
2015	5 33	−69 20	VI	very large, many stars
2027	5 35	−66 59	VI	very large, stars 9th to 11th magnitude
2031	5 36	−66 57	VI	very large, many stars
2099	5 46	32 31	II, III	quite compressed, exceedingly large number of stars
2118	5 48	−69 10	VI	very bright, globular
2164	5 59	−68 31	VI	very bright, globular, easily resolved
2168	6 3	24 21	II, III	very large, many stars
2244	6 27	4 56	II, III	about 12 *Monocerotis*
2287	6 43	−20 38	II, III	very large, bright
2301	6 47	0 35	III	large, many stars
2323	6 58	− 8 12	III	very large, many stars
2360	7 13	−15 27	III	very large, many stars
2422	7 32	−14 16	III	bright, very large, many stars
2437	7 37	−14 35	III	very bright, very large, very many stars
2447	7 40	−23 38	III	large, stars 8th to 13th magnitude
2451	7 42	−37 44	III	exceedingly large, stars about *e Puppis*
2477	7 49	−38 17	III	bright, large, many stars
2506	7 55	−10 21	III	quite large, very rich in faint stars
2516	7 57	−60 36	VI	very bright, very large, stars 7th to 13th magnitude
2539	8 6	−12 32	III	very large, many stars
2547	8 8	−48 58	VI	bright, large
2632	8 34	20 20	III	*Præsepe* in *Cancer*, visible to the naked eye
2682	8 46	12 11	III	very bright, very large, exceedingly large number of stars
2808	9 10	−64 27	VI	very large, very many stars, globular
2932	9 32	−46 30	VI	exceedingly large, very many stars
3114	9 59	−59 38	VI	exceedingly large, stars 9th to 14th magnitude
3532	11 2	−58 8	VI	exceedingly large, round
3766	11 32	−61 2	VI	very large, 150–200 stars
4147	12 5	19 6	III, IV	very bright, quite large, globular, easily resolved
4755	12 48	−59 48	VI	very large, about *κ Crucis*
5024	13 8	18 42	IV	bright, very compressed, globular
5045	13 10	−62 53	VI	very large, very many stars
5139	13 21	−46 47	VI	exceedingly brilliant, *ω Centauri*, visible to naked eye
5272	13 38	28 53	IV	very bright, very large, vast number of stars

No. N. G. C.	Right Ascension	Declination	Map	Description
5822	14 h 38 m	−53° 57′	VI	very large, many stars
5904	15 13	2 27	IV	very bright, large, many stars
5986	15 40	−37 27	IV	very bright, large
6067	16 5	−53 57	VI	very bright, very large, very many stars
6087	16 11	−57 39	VI	bright, large, stars 7th to 10th magnitude
6093	16 11	−22 44	IV	very bright, large, globular, easily resolved
6169	16 27	−43 50	IV, VI	about μ Normæ
6171	16 27	−12 50	IV	large, very many stars, easily resolved
6205	16 38	36 39	IV	very bright, vast number of faint stars
6218	16 42	− 1 46	IV	very bright, very large, easily resolved
6227	16 45	−41 3	IV, VI	exceedingly large, very rich in stars
6254	16 52	− 3 57	IV	bright, very large, easily resolved
6259	16 54	−44 31	IV, VI	bright, very large, very many stars
6266	16 55	−29 58	IV	very bright, large, globular, easily resolved
6333	17 13	−18 25	IV	bright, large, globular, easily resolved
6341	17 14	43 15	I, IV	very bright, very large, globular, easily resolved
6402	17 32	− 3 11	IV, V	bright, very large, very many stars, globular
6444	17 44	−34 50	IV, V	very large, very many stars
6475	17 48	−34 47	IV, V	very bright, many stars
6494	17 51	−19 0	IV, V	bright, very large, many stars
6523	17 57	−24 23	IV, V	very bright, very large
6568	18 7	−21 37	IV, V	very large, stars of 10th magnitude
6603	18 13	−18 27	IV, V	very many stars, visible to naked eye
6611	18 13	−13 49	IV, V	many stars
6626	18 18	−24 55	IV, V	very bright, large, easily resolved
6633	18 23	6 29	IV, V	many bright stars, visible to naked eye
6656	18 30	−23 59	IV, V	very bright, very large, very many stars, globular
6705	18 46	− 6 23	V	very bright, large
6752	19 2	−60 8	VI	bright, very large, easily resolved
6838	19 49	18 31	V	very large, very many stars
6866	20 0	43 43	I, V	large, very many stars
6885	20 8	26 10	V	very bright, very large, stars 6th to 11th magnitude
6940	20 30	27 58	V	very bright, very large, very many stars
7078	21 25	11 44	V	very bright, very large, easily resolved
7089	21 28	− 1 16	V	bright, very large, easily resolved
7092	21 29	48 0	I	very large, stars 7th to 10th magnitude
7099	21 35	−23 38	V	bright, large, globular
7243	22 11	49 23	I	large, bright stars
7654	23 20	61 3	I	large, many stars
7789	23 52	56 10	I	very large, very many stars

TABLE V. — NEBULÆ.

No. N. G. C.	Right Ascension	Declination	Map	Description
55	0 h 10 m	−39° 46′	II, V	very bright, very large, very much elongated
221	0 37	40 19	I, II	exceedingly bright, large, round
224	0 37	40 43	I, II	exceedingly bright, large and elongated
253	0 43	−25 51	II, V	exceedingly bright, large and elongated
598	1 28	30 9	II	very bright, very large, round
613	1 29	−29 55	II	very bright, very large, very much elongated
650	1 36	51 4	I	very bright } double nebula
651	1 36	51 5	I	very bright } double nebula
936	2 23	− 1 35	II	very bright, very large
1023	2 34	38 38	II	very bright, very large and elongated
1365	3 30	−36 32	II	very bright, very large and elongated
1535	4 10	−13 0	II	very bright, small, planetary
1559	4 16	−63 2	VI	very bright, very large and elongated

No. N. G. C.	Right Ascension	Declination	Map.	Description.
1763	4 h. 57 m.	− 66° 34′	VI	very bright, very large
1952	5 28	21 57	II, III	very bright, very large and elongated
1976	5 30	− 5 27	II, III	great nebula about θ *Orionis*
1977	5 30	− 4 54	II, III	about ε *Orionis*
1978	5 28	− 66 18	VI	very bright, very large, oval
1982	5 31	− 5 20	II, III	very bright, very large
1990	5 31	− 1 16	II, III	very large, about ε *Orionis*
2024	5 37	− 1 54	II, III	bright, very large
2070	5 39	− 69 9	VI	very bright, very large, looped
2392	7 23	21 7	III	bright, small, round
2403	7 27	65 49	I	quite bright, very large and elongated
2683	8 46	33 48	III	very bright, very large and elongated
2841	9 45	51 24	I	very bright, large and much elongated
2867	9 49	− 57 53	VI	very small, planetary
3031	9 47	69 32	I	exceedingly bright and large
3115	10 0	− 7 14	III	very bright, large and much elongated
3132	10 3	− 39 57	III	very bright, very large, oval
3199	10 13	− 57 28	VI	very bright, very large
3242	10 20	− 18 8	III	very bright, blue tint, planetary
3372	10 41	− 59 9	VI	diffused and branching about η *Carinæ* (*Argus*)
3379	10 43	13 6	III	very bright, quite large
3587	11 9	55 34	I	very bright, very large, planetary
3623	11 14	13 38	III	bright, very large
3918	11 45	− 56 37	VI	small, round, blue tint, planetary
4254	12 14	14 59	III, IV	bright, large, round, three-branched spiral
4258	12 14	47 52	I	very bright, very large and elongated
4382	12 20	18 45	III, IV	very bright, quite large and round
4565	12 31	26 32	III, IV	bright, very large and elongated
4594	12 35	− 11 4	III, IV	very bright, very large and elongated
4595	12 35	28 31	III, IV	very bright, very large and elongated
4631	12 37	33 16	III, IV	very bright, very large and elongated
4736	12 46	41 40	I, IV	very bright, large
4826	12 52	22 43	IV	very bright, very large and elongated
5128	13 20	− 12 30	IV, VI	very bright, very large and elongated
5194	13 26	47 42	I	great spiral nebula
5236	13 31	− 29 21	IV	very bright, very large, three-branched spiral
5367	13 52	− 39 30	IV	very bright, very large and elongated
6210	16 40	23 59	IV	very bright, very small, planetary
6326	17 13	− 51 38	VI	bright, small, planetary
6369	17 23	− 23 41	IV, V	bright, small, annular
6514	17 56	− 23 2	IV, V	very bright, very large, trifid
6523	17 57	− 24 23	IV, V	very bright, very large, in cluster
6543	17 58	66 38	I	very bright, small, planetary
6572	18 7	6 50	IV, V	very bright, small, planetary
6618	18 15	− 16 13	IV, V	bright, very large, two-hooked
6720	18 50	32 54	IV, V	bright, quite large, annular
6853	19 55	22 27	V	very bright, very large, double condensation
6905	20 18	19 47	V	bright, small, planetary
6960	20 42	30 21	V	quite bright, large, around κ *Cygni*
7009	20 59	− 11 46	V	very bright, small, elliptical
7662	23 21	41 59	I	very bright, small, blue tint, planetary

NOTES TO TABLES IV AND V.

221. Companion nebula to the Great Nebula in Andromeda.

224. THE GREAT NEBULA IN ANDROMEDA. It is plainly visible to the naked eye, and is the brightest nebula in the heavens. It has a nucleus and dark streaks which in the photographs are curved as if indicating a spiral structure.

869, 884. These two clusters are visible to the naked eye and are designated *h* and χ *Persei*, respectively. They are magnificent clusters when viewed with a low-power eyepiece.

1952. The Crab Nebula. It is so named from its appearance in Lord Rosse's reflector.

1976. The Great Nebula in Orion. It surrounds θ *Orionis*, which is visible to the naked eye as a single star, and in the telescope forms the group of four principal stars and two fainter ones known as the trapezium. The nebula is the largest in the sky and has a great rift in it, and also several extensions of irregular shape. A large number of faint stars are involved in the nebula.

3372. The Nebula around η Carinæ (Argus). This is in a region containing many stars forming an immense cluster involved in nebulous matter. The star η *Carinæ*, now of about seventh magnitude, was of extraordinary brilliancy in 1843, exceeded only by *Sirius*; it fluctuated very much in brightness between 1800 and 1870.

5139. This cluster, visible to the naked eye and known as ω *Centauri*, is probably the most magnificent in the sky. It contains several thousand stars.

5194. The Great Spiral Nebula. It was so named by Lord Rosse. It is not very conspicuous in small telescopes, and its structure is distinguishable only in the largest instruments.

6205. This cluster, often called the Great Cluster in Hercules, is perhaps the most magnificent visible to northern observers. It is very densely packed with faint stars.

6514. The Trifid Nebula. It contains several dark rifts, and there is evidence that the nebula has moved, from the change in position of a star with regard to one of these rifts.

6618. The Horseshoe Nebula. It shows this shape only in large instruments.

6720. The Ring Nebula in Lyra. This is the brightest of the circular nebulæ whose condensation is around the circumference of the nebula instead of at its centre.

6853. The Dumbbell Nebula. It was so called by Lord Rosse from its double condensation.

7009. Sometimes called the Saturn Nebula, from a ring seen within the nebula in large telescopes.

In addition to the clusters of Table IV, the whole Milky Way abounds in regions in which the stars are closely compressed, and a telescope with a low-power eyepiece will reveal many brilliant star groups. The naked-eye cluster, the *Pleiades*, also abounds in fainter stars, more than a thousand having been counted and the photographs showing a nebulous background in addition.

THE COLORS OF STARS.

The stars vary in color from red to blue, according to their physical condition. The red stars are in many cases variable. The estimates of color by different observers are often very conflicting, as they depend not only upon the true color of the star, but also upon the condition of the atmosphere, the color imperfection of the telescope used, and the sensitiveness of the observer's eye to differences of tint. Moreover as the star appears as a mere point of light, the color does not seem as pronounced as the word used to express it suggests.

In this atlas, stars of a red color are indicated by the letter *R* placed as a sub-script to the letter or number designating the star. If the star has no letter or number the *R* is placed in parenthesis. Other colors than red are not indicated. The following table contains the stars which are charted as red, in which the color is especially marked, and also a few of other colors which are noteworthy.

Table VI. — Prominent Colored Stars.

Name.	Right Ascension.		Declination.		Magnitude.	Map.	Color.
δ Andromedæ	0ʰ	34ᵐ	30°	19'	3	II, V	Orange
R Sculptoris	1	22	−33	4	var.	II	Red
α Eridani	1	34	−57	44	1	VI	Red
γ Andromedæ	1	58	41	51	2	I, II	Orange
ο Ceti	2	14	− 3	26	var.	II	Red at maximum
R Trianguli	2	31	33	50	var.	II	Red
α Ceti	2	57	3	42	3	II	Orange
— Eridani	4	30	− 9	10	6	II	Red
α Tauri	4	30	16	19	1	II	Red
R Doradus	4	36	−62	16	var.	VI	Red
δ Orionis	4	48	2	21	6	II	Orange
R Leporis	4	55	−14	57	var.	II	Very red
ζ Aurigæ	4	56	40	56	4	I, II	Orange
α Orionis	5	47	7	23	var.	II, III	Red
δ Lyncis	6	18	58	29	6	I	Very red
— Aurigæ	6	30	38	31	6	II, III	Very red
μ Canis Majoris	6	51	−13	54	5	III	Very red
L² Puppis	7	10	−44	29	var.	III, VI	Very red
— Puppis	7	29	−14	18	5	III	Very red
— Mali	9	4	−25	27	5	III	Red
R Leonis	9	42	11	54	var.	III	Red
U Hydræ	10	33	−12	52	var.	III	Red
μ Argus	10	42	−48	54	3	VI	Red
— Centauri	12	37	−48	16	5	VI	Very red
R Hydræ	13	22	−22	32	var.	IV	Red
R Centauri	14	9	−59	27	var.	VI	Red
α Bootis	14	11	19	42	0	IV	Yellow
— Trianguli Australis	15	5	−69	42	5	VI	Red
β Libræ	15	12	− 9	1	3	IV	Pale green
δ¹ Lupi	15	16	−35	54	3	IV	Very red
X Herculis	16	0	47	31	var.	I	Red
— Scorpii	16	2	−26	3	5	IV	Red
α Scorpii	16	23	−26	13	1	IV	Very red
α¹ Herculis	17	10	14	31	3	IV	Orange
γ Draconis	17	54	51	30	2	I	Orange
4 Vulpeculæ	19	21	19	37	5	V	Orange
R Cygni	19	34	49	58	var.	I	Red
χ Cygni	19	47	32	40	var.	V	Red
T Cephei	21	8	68	5	var.	I	Red
μ Cephei	21	40	58	19	var.	I	Red
8 Andromedæ	23	13	48	28	5	I	Red
19 Piscium	23	41	2	56	5	II, V	Red
R Cassiopeiæ	23	53	50	50	var.	I	Red
30 Piscium	23	57	− 6	34	5	II, V	Red

VARIABLE STARS.

In this atlas are included variable stars whose brightness at their maximum equals the sixth magnitude, and also temporary stars which at their brightest were visible to the naked eye but now require a telescope or are wholly invisible. They are indicated by the letter V placed as a subscript to the letter or number designating the star; if the star has no letter or number the letter V is placed in parenthesis. Variable stars, if not already lettered, are designated by the later letters of the alphabet, beginning with R, followed by the Latin genitive of the constellation. They are lettered in the order of their discovery, and after Z is reached the letters are repeated in pairs, RR, RS, etc.

The star symbol used on the maps corresponds with the maximum brightness, except in the case of temporary stars now invisible to the naked eye. The following table contains those charted, with notes regarding the changes in brightness which they experience. The list is made from Chandler's Second Catalogue of Variable Stars.[1] The numbers in the first column are those of that catalogue. Stars of the *Algol*-type are those which are usually at their maximum brightness, but which periodically decrease to a minimum and return again to the maximum.

The variability of the light of stars is of especial interest, because it must be accounted for in any theory of the physical state of the stars. Slow changes in the amount of light given out are to be expected, but periodical changes require special explanation. The greatest interest attaches to stars of the *Algol*-type, which are most naturally accounted for by the periodic passing between us and the star of an eclipsing body. That such a body exists in the case of *Algol* has been proved by the periodic displacement of the lines in the spectrum of the star, so that the star and its companion really form a binary, the two revolving around their common centre of gravity. Another class of variables exhibits the light change in a manner precisely the reverse of that of the *Algol* stars, the star remaining at its minimum brightness the greater part of the time and periodically increasing to a maximum. The periods are not always the same, nor is the brightness at the successive maxima uniform, so that the explanation of this type of variability is not simple and is at present quite conjectural. Another class of variables shows continuous changes in the light, now increasing and now decreasing, the star not remaining at all at any definite degree of brightness. The successive maxima and minima and the rates of change are often variable also, so that the phenomenon is very complicated. Other stars occasionally fluctuate in brightness, but not in any distinct period which can be determined. Another class of variables includes the New or Temporary Stars, improperly so called because they are not new creations, and it is only the great increase of light which is temporary. In every case the light increases rapidly to a maximum, and decreases more slowly, with fluctuations that are remarkably irregular and accompanied by changes in the star's spectrum whose explanation is wholly conjectural.

[1] The Astronomical Journal, Nos. 300, 347, 359.

TABLE VII. — VARIABLE STARS.

No.		Name	Right Ascension	Declination	Map	Maximum Brightness	Minimum Brightness	Period, Days	Notes
100	T	Ceti	0h 17m	—20° 37'	II, V	5.1—5.3	6.4—7.0		occasionally periodic, 60-70 days, at other times irregular
112	R	Andromedae	0 19	38 1	II, V	5.6—8.6	<12.8	411	Sometimes secondary phases, one or two months after maximum
116	B	Cassiopeiae	0 19	63 36	I	>1	?		New star of 1572, observed by Tycho Brahe
209	α	Cassiopeiae	0 35	55 59	I	2.2	2.8		Irregular
224	S	Andromedae	0 37	40 43	I, II	7	0?		New star of 1885 in great nebula of Andromeda
494	R	Sculptoris	1 22	—33 4	II	5.7	7.6—8.0	208	
896	o	Ceti	2 14	—3 26	II	1.7—5.0	8—9.5	332	
996	R	Trianguli	2 31	33 50	II	5.8	11.7	262	
1072	β	Persei	2 59	38 27	II	3.4	4.2		Irregularly periodic
1090	β	Persei	3 2	40 34	I, II	2.3	3.5		Period 2d 20h 49m. Algol. Light oscillations occupy 9 hours
1411	λ	Tauri	3 55	12 12	II	3.4	4.2		Period 3d 22h 52m. Algol-type. Light oscillations occupy 10 hours
1654	R	Doradus	4 36	—62 16	VI	5.7	6.7		Period about 11 months
1768	ε	Aurigae	4 55	43 40	I, II	3.0	4.5		Irregular
1771	R	Leporis	4 55	—14 57	II	6—7	8.5?	436	Remarkable for its crimson color
1800	W	Orionis	5 0	1 2	II	6	7		
1953	T	Aurigae	5 26	30 22	II, III	4.8	<15		New star of 1892. Brightened again to 9th magnitude in 1893
2008	α	Orionis	5 50	7 23	II, III	1	1.4		Irregularly periodic
2213	η	Geminorum	6 20	22 32	II, III	3.2	3.7—4.2	231	
2279	T	Monocerotis	6 20	7 8	II, III	5.8—6.4	7.4—8.2	27	
2375	S	Monocerotis	6 35	9 59	II, III	4.9	5.4	3	
2509	ζ	Geminorum	6 58	20 43	II	3.7	4.5	10	
2583	L²	Puppis	7 10	—44 29	III, VI	3.3	6.3	137	
2610	R	Canis Majoris	7 15	—16 12	III	5.9	6.7		Period 1d 3h 15m. Algol-type. Light oscillations occupy 5 hours
2676	U	Monocerotis	7 26	—9 34	III	5.9—7.3	6.0—8.0	45	Minima alternately bright and faint
2852	V	Puppis	7 48	—48 58	VI	4.4	5.2	4?	Period short, may be 2 days instead of 4
2946	R	Cancri	8 11	12 2	III	6.0—8.3	<11.7	353	
3409	S	Velorum	9 28	—36 36	VI	3.4	4.4	4?	Period short, exact amount doubtful
3418	R	Carinae	9 30	—62 21	VI	4.3—5.7	9.3—10.0	312	
3493	R	Leonis	9 42	11 54	III	5.2—6.7	9.4—10.0	313	
3495	l	Carinae	9 42	—62 3	VI	3.7	5.2	35	
3637	S	Carinae	10 6	—61 4	VI	6.0	9.0—9.2	149	
3796	U	Hydrae	10 33	—12 52	III	4.5	6.1—6.3		Irregularly periodic?
3825	R	Ursae Majoris	10 38	69 18	I	6.0—8.2	13.2	302	Light curve very variable

No.		Constellation	h	m	°	′		Mag	Mag	Period	Remarks
3847	η	Carinae	10	41	−59	10	VI	>1	7.1		Irregular
4435	s	Centauri	12	19	−48	53	VI	6	?		
4511	T	Ursae Majoris	12	32	60	2	I			257	
4826	R	Hydrae	13	24	−22	46	IV	6.0 — 8.5	12.2 — 13.0	425	
4847	s	Virginis	13	28	−6	41	IV	3.5 — 5.5	9.7	376	
5005	R	Centauri	14	9	−59	27	VI	5.7 — 7.8	12.5	160	
5237	R	Bootis	14	33	27	10	IV	6.0 — 6.3	8.7 — 9.8	223	
5274	W	Bootis	14	39	26	57	IV	5.9 — 7.8	11.3 — 12.2		Irregular
5519	R	Apodis	14	46	−76	15	VI	5.2	6.1		
5371	s	Librae	14	56	−8	7	IV	5.5	6.2		Period 2^d 7^h 51^m. *Algol*-type. Light oscillations occupy 12 hours
5667	R	Coronae	15	44	−28	28	IV	5.0	6.2		Irregular
5677	R	Serpentis	15	46	15	26	IV	5.8	13.0		
5732	T	Coronae	15	55	26	12	IV	5.6 — 7.6	13	357	New star of 1866
5758	X	Herculis	16	0	47	31	I	2.0	9.5		
5826	T	Scorpii	16	11	−22	44	IV	6.0	7.2		New star of 1860 in star cluster 6093
5912	g	Herculis	16	25	42	6	I, IV	7.0	<12		Irregular
6044	S	Herculis	16	47	15	7	IV	4.7 — 5.5	5.4 — 6.0	308	
6083		Ophiuchi	16	54	−12	44	IV	5.9 — 7.5	11.6 — 13		New star of 1848
6181	s	Herculis	17	10	14	30	IV	5.5	12.5		Irregular
6189	U	Ophiuchi	17	1		−19	IV	3.1	3.9		Period 21^h irregular. Light oscillations occupy 5 hours
6392	w	Herculis	17	14	33	12	IV	6.0	6.7		Irregularly periodic
6268	w	Ophiuchi	17	25	−21	24	IV, V	4.6	5.4		New star of 1604
6364	X	Sagittarii	17	41	−27	48	IV, V	>1	?		
6472	W	Sagittarii	17	59	−29	35	IV, V	4	6	7	
6573	Y	Sagittarii	18	16	−18	54	IV, V	4.8	5.8	8	
6613	d	Serpentis	18	22	0	8	IV, V	5.8	6.6	6	
6733	R	Scuti	18	42	−5	49	IV, V	5.0	5.7		Short period
6758	β	Lyrae	18	46	33	15	IV, V	4.7 — 5.7	6.0 — 9.0	71	Minima bright and faint, usually alternating
6700	κ	Pavonis	18	47	−67	22	VI	3.4	4.5	9	Period 12^d 21^h 47^m. Secondary maxima and minima
6794	R	Lyrae	18	52	43	49	I, V	4.0	4.7	46	
6849	R	Aquilae	19	2	−5	5	V	5.9 — 7.4	10.9 — 11.5	351	Secondary fluctuations near maximum
6854	Y	Aquilae	19	2	10	55	V	3.3	5.7		
7045	R	Cygni	19	34	49	58	I	5.9 — 8.0	<14	426	
7101	11	Vulpeculae	19	43	27	4	V	3	?		New star of 1670
7120	X	Cygni	19	32	40		V	4.0 — 6.5	13.5	406	
7124	η	Aquilae	19	47	0	65	V	3.5	4.7	7	
7149	S	Sagittae	19	51	16	22	V	5.6	6.4	8	

TABLE VII. — *Continued.*

No.		Name	Right Ascension	Declination	Mag.	Maximum Brightness	Minimum Brightness	Period, Days	Notes.
7285	P	Cygni	20h 14m	37° 43'	V	3—5	<6	365?	So-called new star of 1600
7450	T	Cygni	20 43	34 0	V	5.5?	6?	4	
7483	T	Vulpeculæ	20 47	27 52	V	5.5	6.5	383	
7609	T	Cephei	21 8	68 5	I	5.2—6.8	9.5—9.9	383	
7734	W	Cygni	21 32	44 56	I, V	5.0—6.3	6.1—6.7	131	
7787	Q	Cygni	21 38	42 23	I, V	3	13.5		New star of 1876
7803	S	Cephei	21 40	58 19	I	4?	5?		Irregularly periodic
7994	R	Piscis Australis	22 12	-30 6	V	5.7?	<11?		
8073	δ	Cephei	22 25	57 34	I	3.7	4.9	5	
8273	β	Pegasi	22 59	27 32	I	2.2	2.7		Irregular
8312	R	Aquarii	23 39	-15 50	II, V	5.8—8.5	11?	387	
8600	R	Cassiopeiæ	23 53	50 50	I	4.8—7.0	9.7—12	429	

DOUBLE STARS.

The double stars in the sky number many thousands. The term is used to include those stars which are within 30″ of each other. The eye cannot separate stars unless the distance of the stars is very much greater than this, so that a telescope is necessary for the examination of these objects.

A distinction must be made between naked-eye doubles and telescopic doubles, the latter only receiving the name Double Stars. The former are two stars whose separation must be several minutes of arc, as ζ *Ursæ Majoris* in the handle of the Dipper, and ϵ *Lyræ.* The former is evidently two stars, but the latter is a severe test for the unaided eye, just as the separation of each of its components into two stars is a good test for a telescope. The main components of ϵ *Lyræ* are distant 3′, about the smallest angle which the eye can distinguish.

A further distinction must be made between Double Stars and Binaries. The former is a generic term, applying to all stars separated by less than 30″. (Some authorities would adopt even a smaller limit, as 15″.) The latter is a specific term, and is limited to such double stars as are proved to form a system, the two stars revolving about their common centre of gravity. The aim of the study of double stars is the detection of binaries, which is accomplished by observing the changes in the relative position of the component stars. The existence of stellar systems is a definite proof of the universality of attraction, as announced by Newton when he formulated the law of gravitation.

In addition to the binaries ocularly revealed by the telescope are those whose components are so near each other that they cannot be distinguished with the telescope. They have been detected by the periodic doubling of the lines of their spectra, and are known as spectroscopic binaries.

In this atlas those double stars only are included the brighter component of which is as bright as the sixth magnitude, and the other as bright as the ninth or tenth magnitude. The list therefore contains those double stars which are seen as single stars with the naked eye, but which may be seen as double with small-sized telescopes. These stars are marked D upon the maps, this letter placed as a subscript to the letter or number designating the star. If the star is without letter or number the D is placed in parenthesis.

The following table contains the most interesting double stars of those charted, compiled from various authorities, with the important facts regarding each. The list includes those which surely form a binary system, and also those which are optically interesting because of contrast of color between their components. The magnitudes of the components are given and the position angle and distance of each pair. The position angle is reckoned from the north point towards the east, the vertex of the angle at the brighter component. The position angles and distances of the stars which are known to be revolving about their common centre of gravity are subject to change; the values given are necessarily approximate, but are sufficient for purposes of identification.

TABLE VIII. — DOUBLE STARS.

Name	Right Ascension	Declination	Map	Magnitudes	Position Angle	Distance	Notes
55 Piscium	0h 35m	20° 57'	II, V	6, 9	195°	6"	Colors strongly contrasted — orange, blue
η Cassiopeiæ	0 43	57 17	I	4, 8	150	6	Binary, period about 200 years. Colors — yellow, purple
66 Piscium	0 49	18 38	II	6, 7	—	1	Probably binary. Distance less than 1"
36 Andromedæ	0 50	23 5	II, V	6, 7	0	1	Probably binary, period about 350 years
ψ¹ Piscium	1 0	20 56	II	6, 6	160	30	Binary
α Ursæ Minoris	1 24	88 46	I	2, 9	215	18	Probably binary
ι Ceti	1 37	—11 48	II	6, 7	90	4	Binary
γ Arietis	1 48	18 48	II	5, 5	0	8	Probably binary
λ Piscium	1 57	2 17	II	4, 5	325	3	Probably binary
γ Andromedæ	1 58	41 51	I, II	2, 5, 6	69; 100	10¼	Triple. BC binary. BC very close, less than 1" apart. AB—orange, blue
6 Trianguli	2 6	29 51	I	5, 6	75	4	Probably binary. Colors — yellow, blue
ζ Cassiopeiæ	2 21	66 57	I	5, 7, 8	260, 110	2, 8	Triple. AB binary
γ Ceti	2 38	2 48	II	4, 7	290	3	Binary. Colors — yellow, blue
ε Arietis	2 44	17 3	II	5, 8, 10	120, 110	3, 25	Triple
π Arietis	2 54	20 57	II	5, 6	200	1	Probably binary
α Fornacis	3 8	—29 23	II	4, 7	320	3	Probably binary
ζ Tauri	3 28	24 7	II	6, 7, 10	230, 60	—, 20	Triple. AB very close, less than 1" apart
32 Eridani	3 49	—3 15	II	5, 6	350	7	Probably binary. Colors — yellow, blue
80 Tauri	4 24	15 25	II	6, 6	15	1	Binary
Σ Camelopardalis	4 32	53 17	L	6, 7	290	1	Binary. Colors — yellow, blue
4 Aurigæ	4 52	37 44	II	6, 8	350	1	Binary
ι Orionis	5 2	8 22	II	6, 7	200	1	Seene text, on account of brightness of A
β Orionis	5 10	8 19	II	0, 9	200	10	Binary
λ Orionis	5 25	8 52	II, III	4, 7	190	—	Probably binary. Distance less than 1"
ο Orionis	5 30	—5 58	II, III	3, 8	140	12	Another companion, 11th magnitude, distant 50"
σ Orionis	5 34	—2 39	II, III	4, 10	85	12	Another companion, 7th magnitude, distant 42"
ζ Orionis	5 36	—1 59	II, III	2, 4	150	2	Another companion, 10th magnitude, distant 56"
11 Monocerotis	6 24	—6 58	I	5, 5, 6	130, 125	7, 10	Triple. AB binary
12 Lyncis	6 37	59 32	II, III	5, 6, 7	130, 300	1, 8	Binary, period 49 years. B too close to be now seen
α Canis Majoris	6 41	—16 34	I	—1, 8	—	—	Binary. Distance much less than 1"
15 Lyncis	6 49	58 34	I	4, 6	—	—	Triple. AB binary
ε Geminorum	6 49	13 19	III	5, 8	169	6	Binary. Colors — yellow, blue
μ Canis Majoris	6 51	—13 34	III	5, 8	340	3	

Star					Class	Mag.			Remarks
δ	Geminorum	7	14	22	30	III	4,8	200	7	Probably binary
α	Geminorum	7	28	32	7	III	2,3	230	6	Binary, period very long
κ	Geminorum	7	38	24	38	III	4,8	230	6	
ζ	Cancri	8	6	17	33	III	5,6,6	100,138	1,5	Triple. Probably a ternary system. AB period 60 years
φ²	Cancri	8	21	27	16	III	6,6	230	5	Binary
ε	Hydrae	9	42	6	49	III	3,8	220	4	Binary. Colors — yellow, blue
σ²	Ursae Majoris	9	2	67	33	L	5,8	250	3	Binary
ξ	Leonis	9	23	9	30	III	5,7	—	—	Binary, period 111 years. Distance less than 1"
φ	Ursae Majoris	9	45	54	33	L	4,6	—	—	Binary. Distance less than 1"
γ	Leonis	10	14	20	21	III	2,4	110	3	Binary. Distance less than 1"
54	Leonis	10	50	25	17	III	4,7	100	7	Binary, period 407 years
ε	Ursae Majoris	11	13	32	6	III,IV	4,5	300	1	Binary, period 61 years
-	Leonis	11	19	11	5	III,IV	4,7	70	3	Binary
57	Ursae Majoris	11	24	39	54	III,IV	5,8	0	6	Binary
90	Leonis	11	30	17	21	III,IV	6,7	210	3	Probably binary. Another companion, 8th magnitude, distant 60"
α	Canum Venaticorum	12	11	41	13	L,IV	6,9	260	11	Colors well contrasted — yellow, blue
2	Crucis	12	21	-62	23	VI	1,2	120	5	Binary. Another companion, 6th magnitude, distant 60"
24	Comae Berenices	12	30	18	56	III,IV	5,7	270	20	Colors strongly contrasted — orange, purple
γ	Centauri	12	36	-48	24	VI	2,4	0	1	Binary
γ	Virginis	12	37	0	54	III,IV	4,4	160	5	Binary, period 185 years
35	Comae Berenices	12	48	21	47	III,IV	5,8,9	60,125	1,28	Triple. AB binary
-	Canum Venaticorum	12	51	38	53	III,IV	3,7	239	20	Another companion, 10th magnitude, distant 65"
θ	Virginis	13	5	-5	0	IV	4,9	345	7	Binary, period 26 years. Distance less than 1"
42	Comae Berenices	13	5	18	4	IV	5,5	190	—	Binary. g (Alcor) 12' distant
ζ	Ursae Majoris	13	20	55	27	L	2,4	150	15	Binary, period 125 years. Distance less than 1"
25	Canum Venaticorum	13	33	36	48	IV	5,8	—	—	Binary
84	Virginis	13	38	4	3	I	6,8	230	3	Binary
κ	Bootis	14	10	52	15	I	4,7	240	13	
ι	Centauri	14	15	0		VI	6,8	163	10	
-	Centauri	14	33	-60	26	VI	1,3	—	2	Binary, period 80 years. Distance now increasing
κ	Bootis	14	36	16	51	IV	5,6	160	6	Probably binary
ζ	Bootis	14	36	14	10	IV	4,5	300	1	Probably binary
ε	Bootis	14	41	27	30	IV	3,6	330	3	Binary
ι	Bootis	14	47	19	31	IV	5,7	280	4	Binary, period uncertain
μ	Lupi	15	0	48	2	I	5,6	240	5	Binary, period 260 years
μ	Lupi	15	12	-47	31	VI	5,7,8	175,130	2,23	Triple
η	Coronae Borealis	15	19	30	38	IV	6,6	90	—	Binary, period 40 years. Distance less than 1"

TABLE VIII. — *Continued.*

Name	Right Ascension	Declination	Map	Magnitudes	Position Angle	Distance	Notes
δ Serpentis	15h 36m	10° 59'	IV	4,5	190	4	Binary
ζ Coronae Borealis	15 30	36 58	IV	5,6	300	6	Binary, period 73 years. Distance much less than 1"
γ Coronae Borealis	15 30	26 37	IV	4,7	120	—	Triple. Binary
β Scorpii	15 59	-11 6	IV	5,6,7	190,65	1,7	
ν Scorpii	16 0	-19 32	IV	3,5	25	14	
σ Scorpii	16 6	-19 12	IV	4,7;7,8	CD 30	CD 2	Quadruple. AB less than 1" apart, probably binary
σ Coronae Borealis	16 11	34 7	IV	5,6	209	3	Binary, period uncertain
η Draconis	16 23	61 44	I	3,8	140	5	
? Scorpii	16 23	-26 13	IV	1,8	275	3	Binary. Colors — orange, green
λ Ophiuchi	16 26	2 13	IV	4,6	30	2	Binary, period 96 years
ζ Herculis	16 38	31 46	IV	3,6	129	1	Binary, period 34 years
? Draconis	17 3	54 36	I	6,6	170	3	Probably binary
α Ophiuchi	17 9	-26 27	IV	4,6	200	5	Binary
η Herculis	17 10	14 31	IV	3,6	115	5	Colors — orange, green
α Herculis	17 11	24 57	IV, V	3,8	180	18	Probably binary
δ Herculis	17 20	37 15	IV, V	4,5	310	4	Binary
95 Herculis	17 57	21 37	IV, V	5,5	260	6	Colors — yellow, blue
τ Ophiuchi	17 58	-8 11	IV, V	5,6	250	2	Binary, period 218 years
70 Ophiuchi	18 0	2 32	IV, V	4,6	300	2	Binary, period 88 years
73 Ophiuchi	18 5	3 58	IV, V	6,7	250	1	Binary
b Draconis	18 23	58 45	I	5,8	0	4	
ε Lyrae	18 41	39 34	IV, V	5,6;5,6	20,140	3,2	Quadruple. Both pairs binary
11 Aquilae	18 54	13 30	V	6,9	200	17	
i Cygni	19 10	49 37	I	6,6	220	10	Binary
β Cygni	19 27	27 45	I	3,5	60	34	Colors strongly contrasted — yellow, blue
δ Cygni	19 42	44 53	I, V	3,8	340	2	Binary, period uncertain
τ Aquilae	19 44	11 34	V	6,7	120	1	
β Delphini	20 33	14 15	V	4,4,11	-,340	-,35	Triple. Binary. AB less than 1" apart
52 Cygni	20 42	30 21	V	4,9	60	6	
γ Delphini	20 42	15 46	V	5,6	276	11	Binary
λ Cygni	20 43	36 7	V	5,6	80	—	Binary. Distance less than 1"
ε Equulei	20 54	3 55	V	5,6,7	280,75	1,10	Triple. Binary
61 Cygni	21 2	38 13	V	6,0	115	20	Binary

						V	5, 5, 10	—.25	—.40	
δ	Equulei	21	10	9	36	V	4, 8	150	1	Triple. Binary. AB very close, period 6–14 years
γ	Cygni	21	11	32	37	V	5, 7			Binary
ι	Iolis	21	13	−53	52	VI	5, 6	120	4	Binary
ψ	Cygni	21	40	28	17	V	4, 1	285	7	Binary
2	Cephei	22	1	64	6	I	4, 5	380	3	Binary, period very long
ψ	Aquarii	22	31	39	32	V	5, 6	185	22	
8	Lacertæ	22	5	0	7	V	4, 7	315	1	Binary
94	Cephei	23	14	−14	50	V	5, 8	345	14	Binary
ο	Aquarii	23	14	67	1	I		190	2	Binary
107	Cephei	23	41	−19	22	II.	8, 7	140	9	
86	Pegasi	23	57	56	13	A. II.	6, 9	50	14	

USE OF THE STAR ATLAS.

The following suggestions are offered for the assistance of those using the atlas for either constellation study or the examination of the sky with the telescope.

DESIGNATION OF STELLAR POSITIONS IN THE SKY.

The method used by astronomers for designating positions of the heavenly bodies should be understood. This is precisely the same as that of designating positions on the earth by their longitude and latitude. Upon the sky, which appears to us as a sphere, one half of whose inner surface is always visible, we must imagine the equator to be drawn and a system of meridians and parallels to be added. The celestial equator is the trace upon the sky which the plane of the earth's equator would make. As we see it from any point of the earth's surface except the poles, it passes through the east and west points of the horizon, and is inclined to the horizon by an angle which is 90° minus the latitude of the place. Where it crosses the meridian, it is distant from the zenith by an angle equal to the latitude of the place. The sun in its daily path across the sky describes the equator at the time of the equinoxes, about March 20th and September 21st; on other days it describes parallels either north or south of the equator.

The pole of the equator is the fixed point in the sky which marks the prolongation of the earth's axis. It is always due north of the observer in the northern hemisphere or due south in the southern hemisphere, and is as many degrees above the horizon as the latitude of the place of observation. Its place is indicated roughly for northern observers by the second magnitude star *a Ursæ Minoris*, or *Polaris*, and for southern observers by the fifth magnitude star *σ Octantis*. The great circles, all of which intersect at the pole and are drawn perpendicular to the equator at its several points, like the meridians on the earth, are called in the sky *hour circles*, not meridians. The term *meridian* is reserved for the circle passing through the pole and the observer's zenith. Each hour circle in turn momentarily coincides with the observer's meridian, as the earth turns on its axis. The parallels to the celestial equator are drawn precisely as upon the earth. They are called parallels of declination instead of parallels of latitude. Each of the heavenly bodies describes the equator or one of these parallels as the daily rotation of the earth on its axis causes it to move across the sky. One of the best ways of fixing the whole system of circles in the mind is to watch the movements of the heavenly bodies for a few hours on some clear night, having first located the east and west points of the horizon and the position of the pole.

Each star in the sky has an hour circle passing through it, just as each point on the earth is upon one of the terrestrial meridians. The distance of the star from the celestial equator is called its *declination*, north or + if the star is north of the equator, and south or − if south of the equator. This corresponds precisely with latitude on the earth. In order to get the other measure corresponding with longitude, it is necessary to select one of the hour circles as a reference circle, just as the meridian passing through Greenwich is chosen on the earth. The hour circle passing through the point on the celestial equator where the sun crosses it in the spring, called therefore the vernal equinox, is selected as the reference hour circle. It is called the *equinoctial colure*. The hour circle at right angles to this, which therefore passes through the sun's solstitial points in summer and winter, is called the *solstitial colure*. The angle between the equinoctial colure and the hour circle passing through any star is called its *right ascension*. It corresponds with longitude on the earth, with the exception that it is reckoned from the equinoctial colure towards the east all the way around the sphere, amounting therefore to 24 hours or 360°, while longitude is reckoned both eastward and westward from the meridian of Greenwich and therefore does not exceed 12 hours or 180°. Right ascension is usually given in hours, minutes, and seconds instead of degrees, minutes, and seconds, just as is frequently done in expressing terrestrial longitudes.

It is a great help to a living appreciation of the system of circles above described and their use in determining the right ascension and declination of the heavenly bodies, if one will take the trouble to estimate the right ascension and declination of any star, and then compare them with the true values given on the chart. To do this it is necessary first to know where the vernal equinox is in the sky, or else the right ascension of some star which can be used instead for reference. In the latter case the difference between the right ascension of the given star and the reference star is estimated, and this difference added to the known right ascension. It is wise to select for these estimates stars in different parts of the sky.

CONSTELLATION STUDY.

An acquaintance with the leading star groups is to be recommended not only for itself, but because it gives a clearer idea of the motion of the earth on its axis and about the sun, and also of lunar and planetary movements. It is well, however, to remember that the tracing of the old figures is no part of modern Astronomy, and that little resemblance is to be sought between the names of the constellations and the stars grouped within them. It is very doubtful if the ancient astronomers who invented this method of designating star groups fancied close resemblances between the groups and the names assigned. In only a few cases, notably those of a snake-like figure, as *Draco, Serpens,* and *Hydra,* is it possible to detect any resemblance whatever. It is also well to recall that the constellations occupy a very humble position in the modern science of Astronomy, as their use is simply the giving of names to areas in the sky.

The chief difficulties to be encountered in studying the constellations arise from their changing positions in the sky due to the earth's daily motion on its axis and its annual motion around the sun. As a result of the former, the same constellation appears tipped at a different angle in one part of the sky than in another a few hours later. As a result of the latter the constellations appear farther westward on any evening than they did at the same time the previous evening. The remedy for these difficulties is to learn the constellations with regard to each other and not with regard to the time of day or of year, and certainly not with regard to terrestrial objects.

The following plan is suggested for a systematic study of the constellations :

1. Divide the heavens into four grand divisions, bounded by the equinoctial and solstitial colures. Trace these colures in the sky by the prominent stars near which they pass. In the northern sky the seven stars of *Ursa Major* known popularly as the Dipper will furnish a beginning. The two stars α and β, forming the side of the bowl of the Dipper and known as the "pointers," will lead to the pole star, α *Ursæ Minoris,* by prolonging the line from β to α to about five times its length. The middle star of the seven, δ *Ursæ Majoris,* at the junction of the handle with the bowl of the Dipper, and the faintest star of the seven, is very near the equinoctial colure. Imagine a line connecting the pole star with δ *Ursæ Majoris.* It is a portion of the equinoctial colure ; if prolonged from the pole star beyond δ *Ursæ Majoris* it will intersect the equator at the autumnal equinox. The star η *Virginis* is not far from this point. If prolonged in the other direction from δ

Ursæ Majoris beyond the pole star it will intersect the equator at the vernal equinox.
There is a line of bright stars easily traced which marks the way, made up of β *Cassiopeiæ*,
α *Andromedæ*, and γ *Pegasi*. The first of these is in the foot of the chair-shaped figure
which is the characteristic figure of *Cassiopeia ;* the second and third form the eastern side of
the conspicuous quadrilateral known as the "Square of Pegasus." The vernal equinox itself is in the relatively starless region south of γ *Pegasi ;* the line from α *Andromedæ* to γ
Pegasi should be prolonged as far beyond the latter as they are apart. After the equinoctial colure has been traced as above, and the vernal and autumnal equinoxes located, the
solstitial colure may be similarly traced at right angles to the above. It will lead nearly to
η *Geminorum* for the summer solstice, and in the reverse direction to μ *Sagittarii* for the
winter solstice.

2. Learn the zodiacal groups. Each of these has a characteristic figure, by which it
may be recognized. The groups are of first importance, because in them lies the ecliptic
or the sun's path through the heavens, and also the paths of the moon and leading planets.
It is advisable to note from the maps just where the ecliptic itself passes among the stars
of these groups.

3. Add the leading constellations north and south of the zodiacal groups, and later
the less conspicuous groups. At first only the leading stars should be noted, the fainter
ones to be added later if desired.

4. Learn the twenty stars usually known as stars of the first magnitude.

The constellations are best learned by their characteristic figures. In order to aid in
this study, six smaller maps precede the main maps of the atlas. Their outlines and
general plan are precisely the same as those of the larger maps. They contain the stars
down to the fourth magnitude, with a few fainter stars where necessary to complete a
characteristic figure. In many cases there is no question as to what constitutes the leading
stellar figure of any constellation area, but in others different observers may sometimes
differ as to the figures. The connecting lines which are drawn upon these maps are
intended as guides to help in tracing the characteristic figures. It is to be expected of
course that different students will oftentimes prefer different arrangements to those here
presented.

The student who is interested in the historical development of the subject may profit-
ably refer to the larger maps and note the outlines of the old figures in their relation to the
actual stellar figures.

In order to facilitate the study of the constellations in an orderly way, a rearrangement of the constellations according to the four divisions of the sky is here given. The
circumpolar constellations of all four divisions can best be studied together, but the equatorial constellations of the four divisions by themselves. For this reason, the maps of this
atlas are arranged as two circumpolar maps, and the intermediate parts of the sky in four
divisions bounded by the equinoctial and solstitial colures. The Roman numerals I, II,
III, and IV refer to the four divisions respectively. The zodiacal constellations are
printed in small capitals, and the other original constellations of Ptolemy's list, which
have the most conspicuous figures in the northern sky, in italics. Where a constellation
area is partly in one and partly in another division, it is here listed in the division in
which the greater part of its area lies.

TABLE IX. — CONSTELLATIONS ARRANGED ACCORDING TO THEIR POSITION IN THE SKY.

NORTHERN POLAR.

I.	II.	III.	IV.
Cassiopeia	Lynx	Ursa Minor	Cygnus
Camelopardalis	Ursa Major	Draco	Lacerta
Perseus			Cepheus
EQUATORIAL I.	EQUATORIAL II.	EQUATORIAL III.	EQUATORIAL IV.
Andromeda	Leo Minor	Coma Berenices	Lyra
Triangulum	Gemini	Canes Venatici	Aquila
Auriga	Cancer	Bootes	Sagitta
Pisces	Leo	Hercules	Vulpecula
Aries	Monoceros	Corona Borealis	Delphinus
Taurus	Canis Minor	Ophiuchus	Equuleus
Cetus	Sextans	Serpens	Pegasus
Eridanus	Hydra	Virgo	Scutum
Orion	Crater	Libra	Sagittarius
Lepus	Canis Major	Scorpius	Capricornus
Sculptor	Argo (Puppis)	Corvus	Aquarius
Fornax	(Malus)	Lupus	Microscopium
Celum	Antlia		Piscis Australis
Columba			

SOUTHERN POLAR.

I.	II.	III.	IV.
Phœnix	Argo (Vela)	Centaurus	Corona Australis
Horologium	(Carina)	Norma	Grus
Hydrus	Volans	Ara	Telescopium
Reticulum	Chamæleon	Crux	Indus
Dorado		Circinus	Tucana
Pictor		Musca	Pavo
Mensa		Triangulum Australe	Octans
		Apus	

The names of the months given at the margins of the star maps show the times of year when the constellations can best be studied in the evening. The names are placed beneath the hour circles which correspond with the meridian at 9 P.M. local time. On the circumpolar maps the names are placed under the hour circles which extend from the pole downward to the horizon at the time named. To illustrate, — suppose that the heavens are to be examined October 1st, 9 P.M. Map V shows that at that time the hour circle which marks the right ascension, 21 h. 40 min., nearly coincides with the meridian. The constellations west of the meridian are those west of this hour circle and are given on Map V; those east of the meridian are partly on Map V and Map II. Map I shows how the northern constellations appear to a person in the northern hemisphere when the page is turned so that the date is at the bottom. *Cassiopeia* is below the pole towards the left, *Ursa Major* high in the sky above the pole. The following table is given to aid still further in determining the position of the constellations at different times of the year. It gives the right ascensions which coincide with the meridian at 9 P.M. on the dates named.

TABLE X. — SIDEREAL TIME AT 9 P.M., OR RIGHT ASCENSION OF THE HOUR CIRCLE WHICH COINCIDES WITH THE MERIDIAN OF THE OBSERVER.

January	1	3ʰ 45ᵐ	April	1	9ʰ 39ᵐ	July	1	15ʰ 38ᵐ	October	1	21ʰ 41ᵐ
	15	4 49		15	10 34		15	16 33		15	22 36
February	1	5 47	May	1	11 37	August	1	17 40	November	1	23 43
	15	6 42		15	12 33		15	18 35		15	0 38
March	1	7 37	June	1	13 40	September	1	19 42	December	1	1 41
	15	8 32		15	14 35		15	20 38		15	2 36

The maps giving the constellations near the equator, Maps II–V, are arranged with the west toward the right and the east toward the left, just as the sky appears to a person in the northern hemisphere when facing south. If the atlas is used in the southern hemisphere, the page is to be inverted. The equator is drawn as a horizontal line; it must be remembered that in the sky it is a semicircle which extends from the eastern point of the horizon to the western point, and that where it crosses the meridian it is distant from the zenith by an amount equal to the observer's latitude. Therefore, if the map is held so that the hour circle which is on the meridian is nearly vertical, the equator at both the left and the right will gradually approach the horizon, touching it at hour circles six hours greater and less than that on the meridian. If one views the constellations facing the east or west, he may turn the atlas so that the equator as drawn will make an angle with the vertical equal to the latitude of the place, and the star groups will appear at about the angle which they have in that part of the sky.

TELESCOPIC STUDY.

The atlas is designed to assist those with small telescopes who may desire to find objects in the sky. For this reason, in addition to the stars readily visible without a telescope, the leading clusters, nebulæ, double stars, red stars, and variables have been located on the maps. The number of stars of the fainter magnitudes visible in a telescope of only 2 inches aperture is so large that they could not be charted without crowding the maps. The stars charted can be seen with the naked eye and examined themselves, or used as starting-points from which to find the other objects charted. The lists given in the preceding pages contain the leading objects of each class in the sky.

It is well to know what can be expected of any given telescope. One of 2 inches aperture will show stars as faint as the 10th magnitude ; of 4 inches aperture, as faint as the 12th magnitude ; of 10 inches aperture, as faint as the 14th magnitude. But stars on the extreme limit of brightness thus stated can be seen only when atmospheric conditions are good and the instrument well focussed for the observer's eye. The dividing power of a telescope in the examination of double stars depends upon the magnifying power used and also upon the steadiness of the atmosphere and the magnitudes of the components. The magnifying power of the telescope under ordinary atmospheric conditions is rarely more than 20 or 30 times the aperture of the telescope in inches. Familiarity with the instrument and its different eyepieces will show the observer what eyepieces are best adapted for use under different conditions. Double stars, the distance of whose components is less than 2″ or 3″, are difficult objects for the amateur to divide with telescopes under 6 inches aperture, especially if the components are bright. The quadruple star ε *Lyræ* is an excellent object with which to test the capacity of the telescope for this kind of observing.

In order to use the star chart to find objects invisible to the naked eye, when the telescope is not provided with setting circles, it is well to know the diameter of the field of view in minutes of arc. This will differ for different eyepieces, diminishing as the magnifying power increases. It can be determined in several ways, as (1) by estimating the diameter of the field in terms of the diameter of the moon seen with the given eyepiece. The moon's diameter is about $32'$. (2) By determining the time which it takes a star to move centrally across the field, the telescope remaining at rest. If the star is near the equator and the time is expressed in minutes and a fraction, simply multiplying by 15 will give the diameter of the field in minutes of arc. If the star is not near the celestial equator, the resulting value will be too large and must be multiplied by the cosine of the star's declination. When the diameter of the field is known, it is easy to move the telescope from a star towards which the telescope may be directed a sufficient amount to bring the desired object into the field. If the object, for instance a nebula, is on the star map, its distance and direction from a star visible to the naked eye may be estimated, and the former converted into diameters of the field of the telescope. If an object not upon the map is to be examined, for instance a comet, it may be located upon the map by its right ascension and declination, and then its relation to some star determined.

Nebulæ are usually disappointing objects in a small telescope. The descriptions published describe them as they appear in very large instruments. Very few of them are sufficiently bright to show much detail of structure unless the telescope is of at least 12 inches aperture.

The colors of stars are usually not so marked in the telescope as one might expect. The uncorrected color of the telescope itself and the color added by the atmosphere, especially if the star is near the horizon, give a spurious tint which must not be confounded with the real color of the star. It is also very necessary for noting colors of the star that the telescope should be well focussed. The stars marked red are usually of a less pronounced shade of red than the word might seem to indicate.

In the use of a telescope too little attention is often given to the firmness of the support of the telescope and to a careful focussing for the individual eye of the observer. Care in these matters will enable the observer to use the instrument to better advantage, and experience will often show that its capabilities are much greater than at first supposed.

CHARACTERISTIC CONSTELLATION FIGURES.

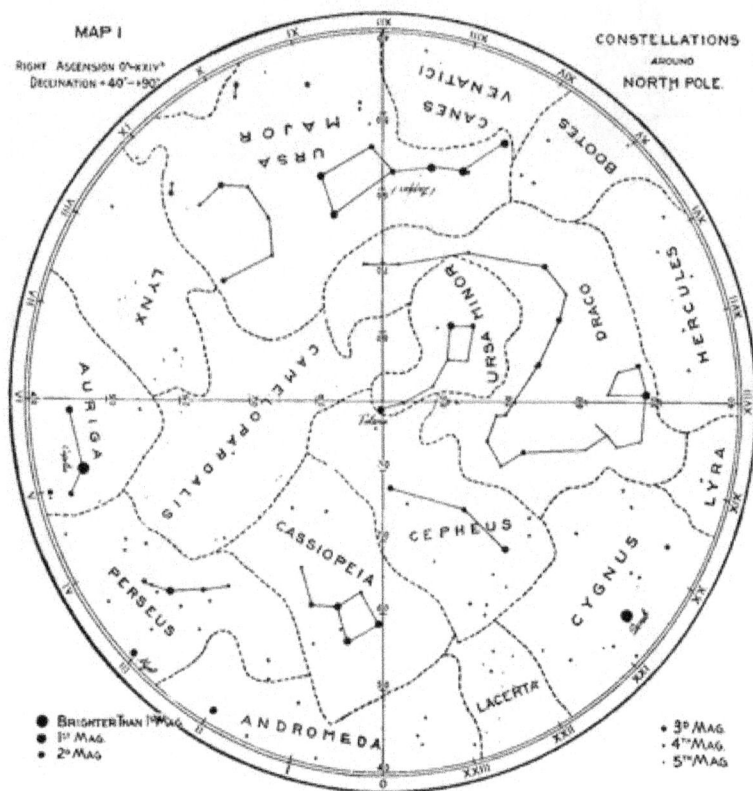

MAP I

RIGHT ASCENSION 0ʰ–xxiv
DECLINATION +40°–+90°

CONSTELLATIONS
AROUND
NORTH POLE.

AURIGA   PERSEUS   ANDROMEDA

GEMINI   TRIANGULUM   PEGASUS

TAURUS   ARIES   PISCES

ORION

MONOCEROS   CETUS   AQUARIUS

LEPUS   ERIDANUS

CANIS MAJOR   FORNAX   SCULPTOR

COLUMBA   CAELUM   PHOENIX

ARGO   HOROLOGIUM

CANES VENATICI   URSA MAJOR   LYNX   AURIGA

COMA BERENICES   LEO MINOR   GEMINI   TAURUS

LEO   CANCER

VIRGO   CANIS MINOR   ORION

SEXTANS   MONOCEROS

CRATER   HYDRA   CANIS MAJOR   LEPUS

CORVUS   MALUS ARGO   PUPPIS   COLUMBA

ANTLIA

CENTAURUS   VELA

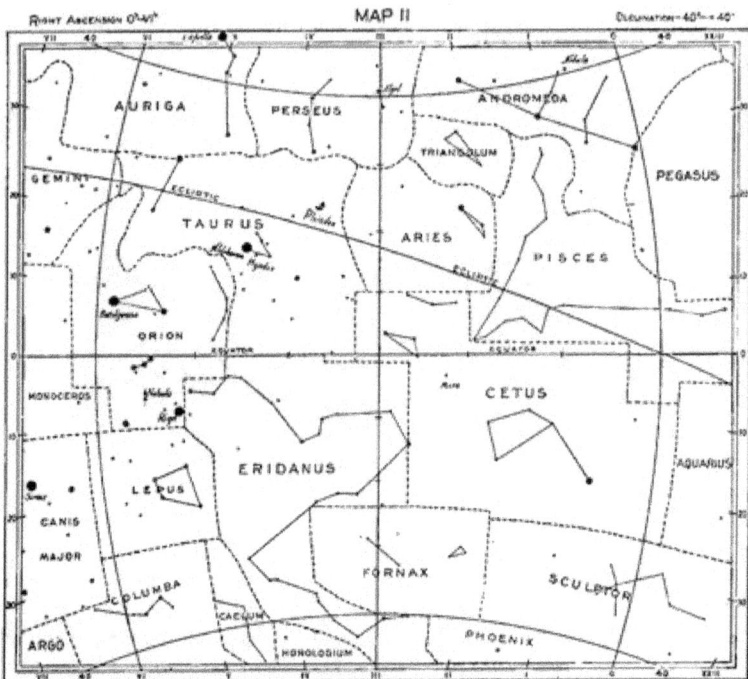

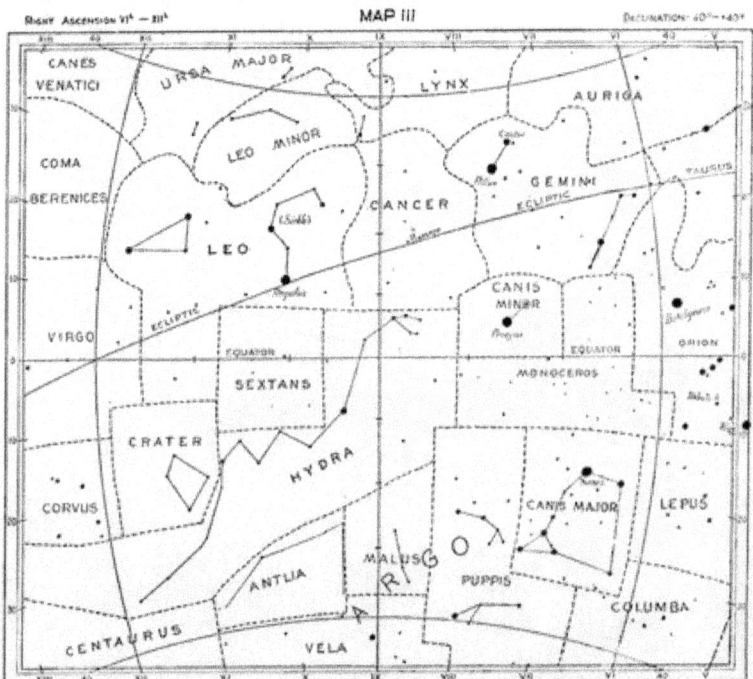

● Brighter than 1ˢᵗ Mag.   ● 1ˢᵗ Mag.   ● 2° Mag.   • 3° Mag.   • 4ᵗʰ Mag.   · 5ᵗʰ Mag.

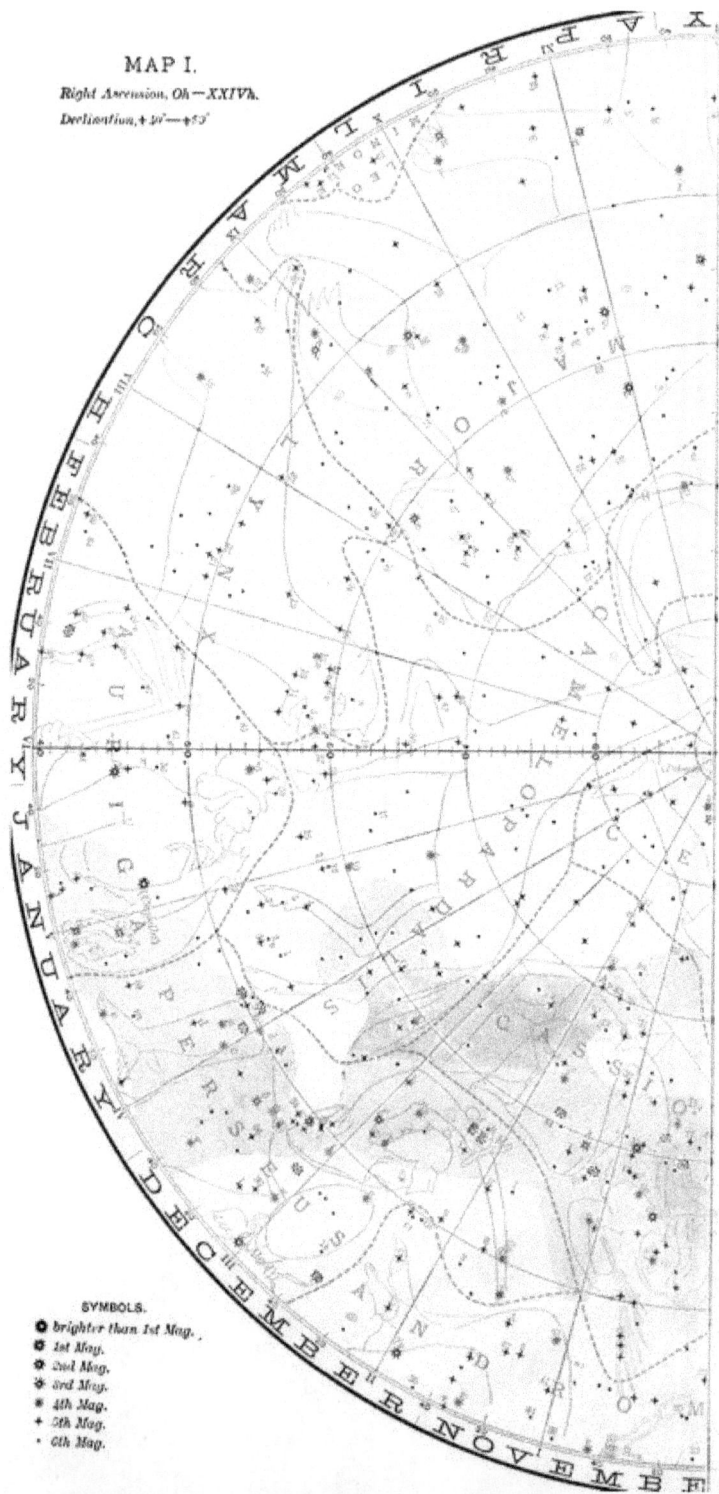

MAP I.

Right Ascension, 0h — XXIVh.

Declination, +20° — +55°

CONSTELLATIONS
AROUND
NORTH POLE

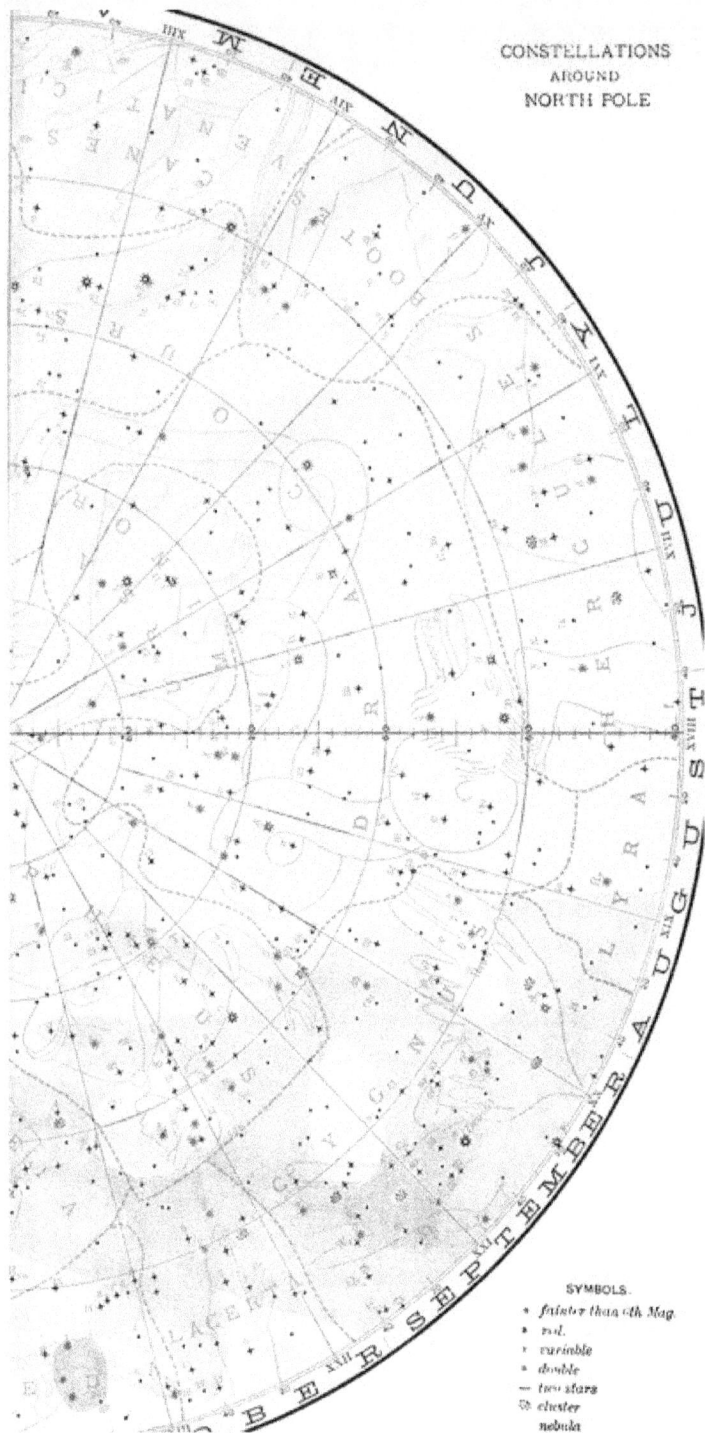

SYMBOLS.
* fainter than 6th Mag.
* red.
* variable
* double
— two stars
* cluster
nebula

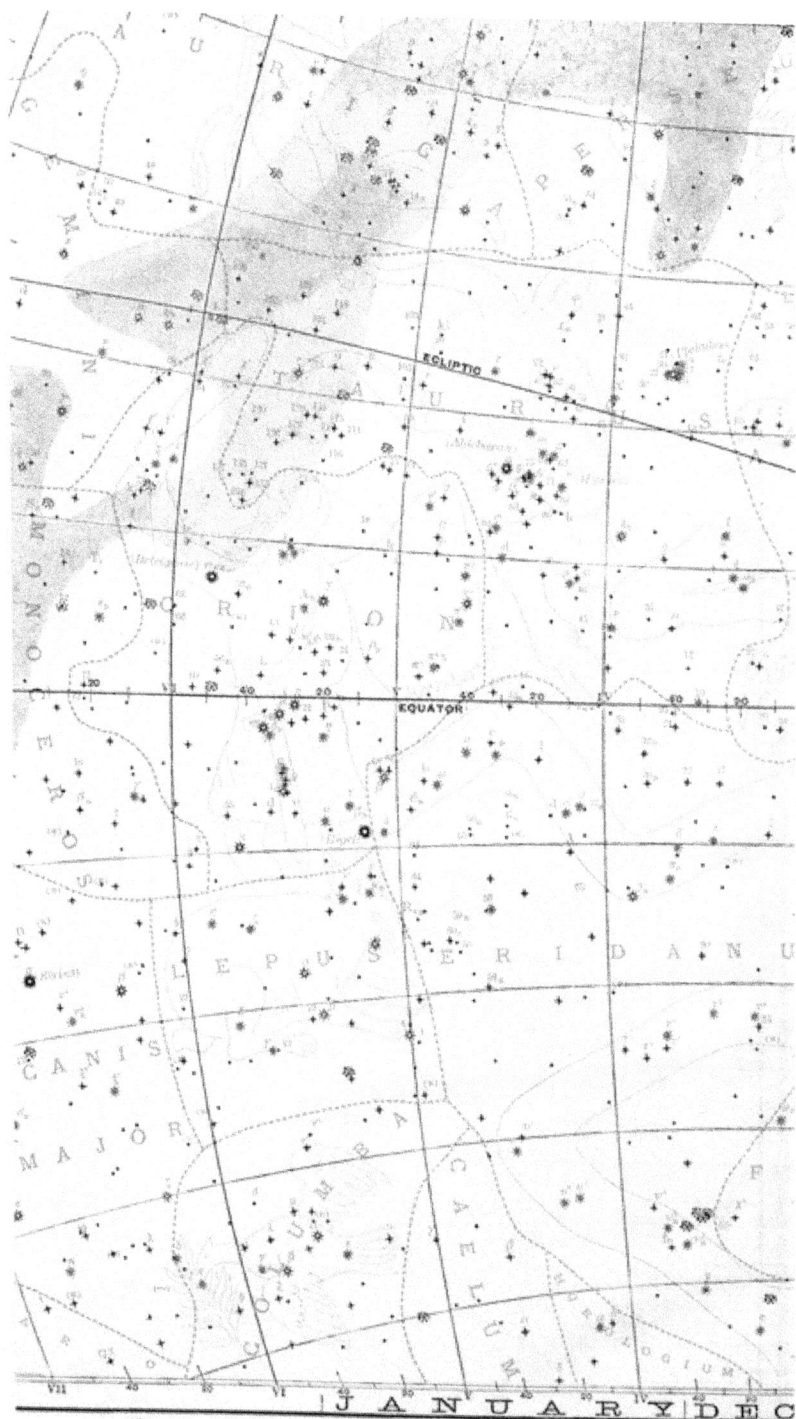

ECLIPTIC

EQUATOR

AURIGA

PERSEUS

TAURUS

ORION

MONOCEROS

LEPUS

ERIDANUS

CANIS

MAJOR

COLUMBA

CAELUM

HOROLOGIUM

VII

JANUARY DEC

○ brighter than 1st Mag.　⊙ 1st Mag.　✸ 2nd Mag.　✸ 3rd Mag.　✳ 4th Mag.　+ 5th Mag.　· 6th M

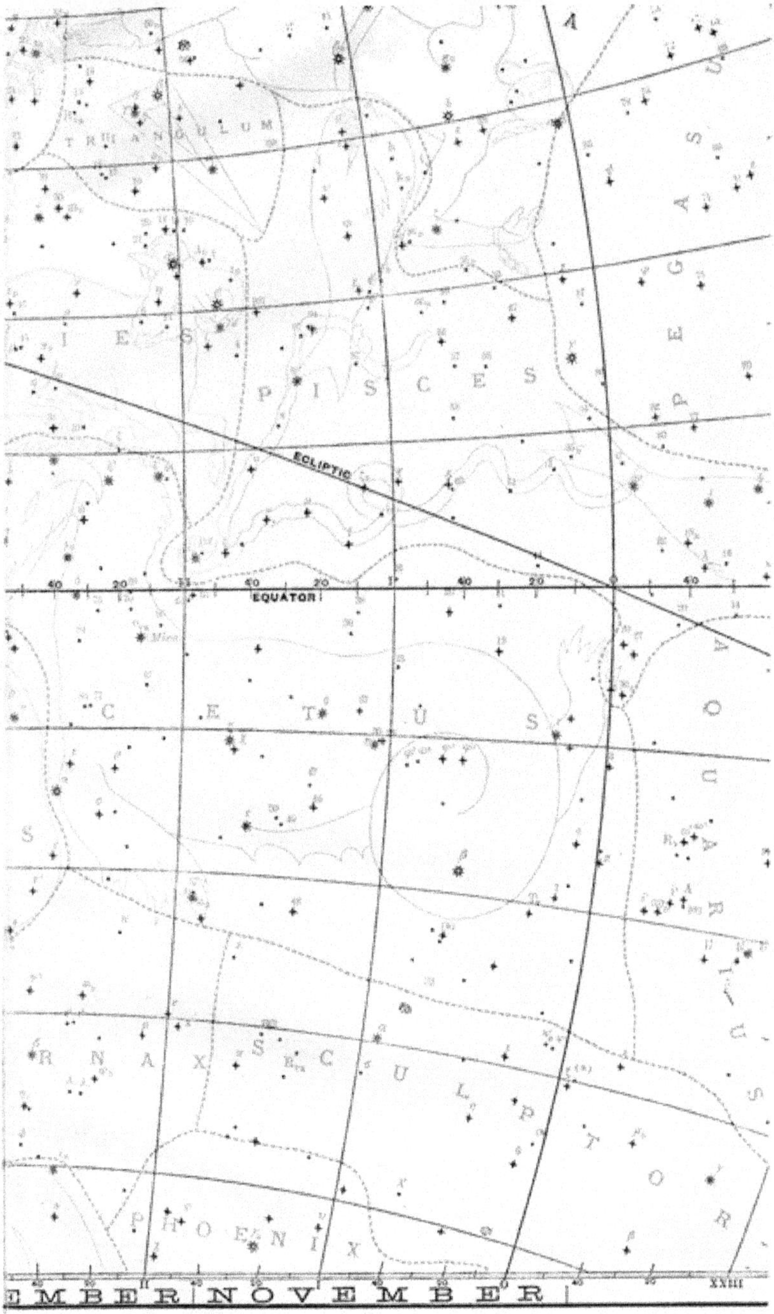

TRIANGULUM

PEGASUS

PISCES

P I S C E S

ECLIPTIC

EQUATOR

40   20   40   20   40   20   40

Mira

C E T U S

AQUARIUS

FORNAX   SCULPTOR

PHOENIX

EMBER NOVEMBER   XXIII

· fainter than 6th Mag.   ჲ red.   v variable.   » double.   — two stars.   ✹ cluster.   ꙮ nebula.

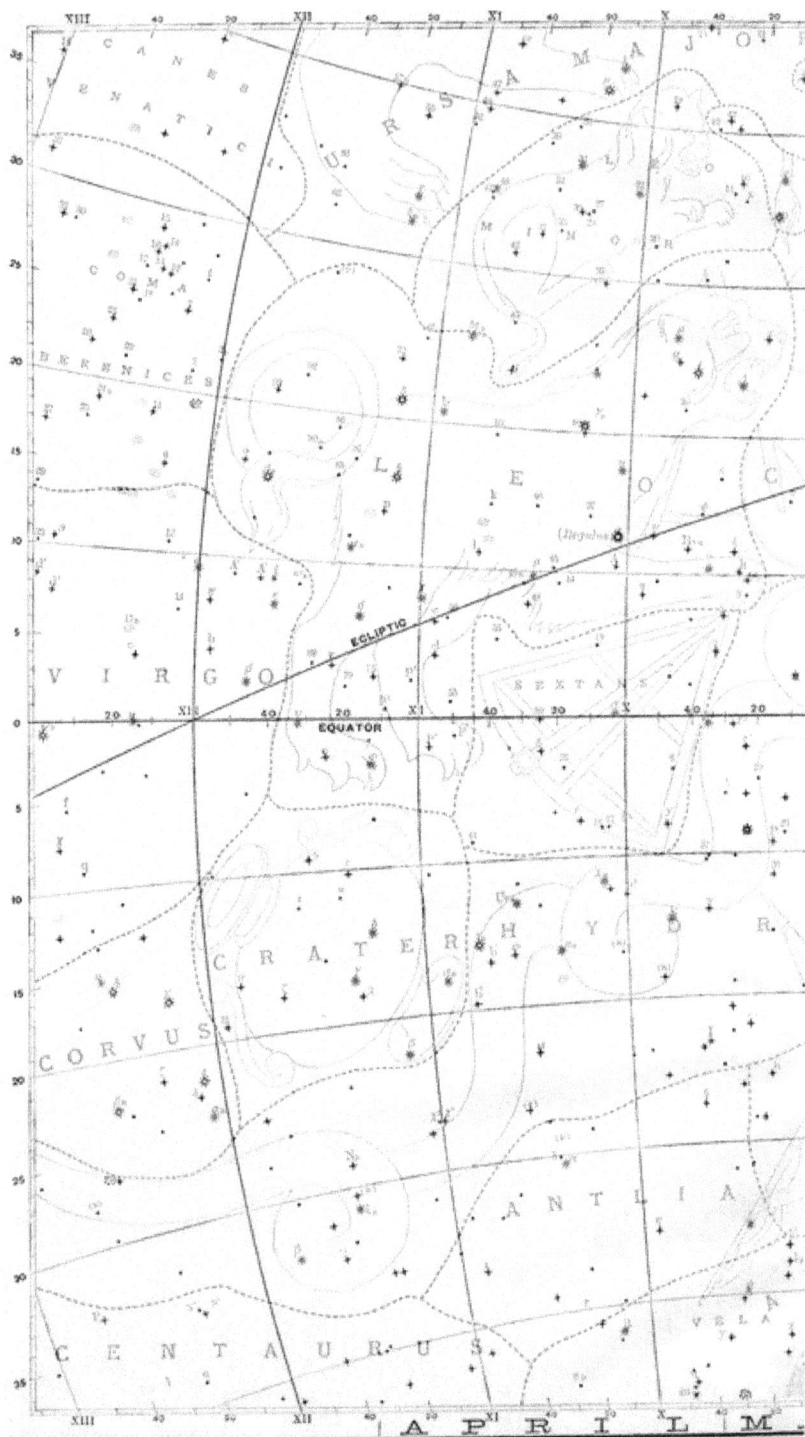

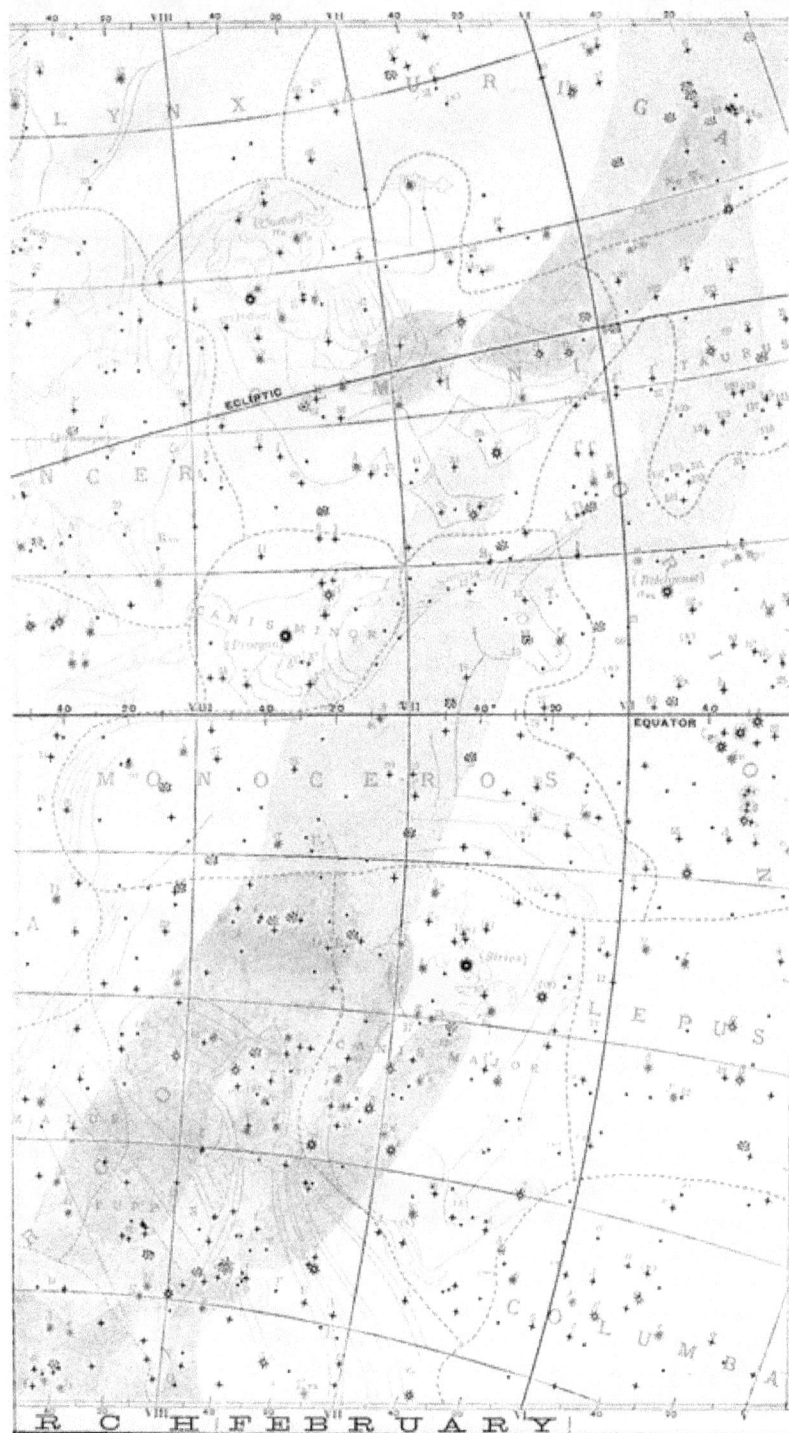

LYNX

AURIGA

X

ECLIPTIC

CANCER

TAURUS

ORION

Betelgeuse

CANIS MINOR

Procyon

EQUATOR

MONOCEROS

Z

Sirius

LEPUS

CANIS MAJOR

COLUMBA

MARCH FEBRUARY

* fainter than 6th Mag.   • red   ▽ variable.   ⋄ double.   — two stars.   ✸ cluster.   ⦿ nebula.

s

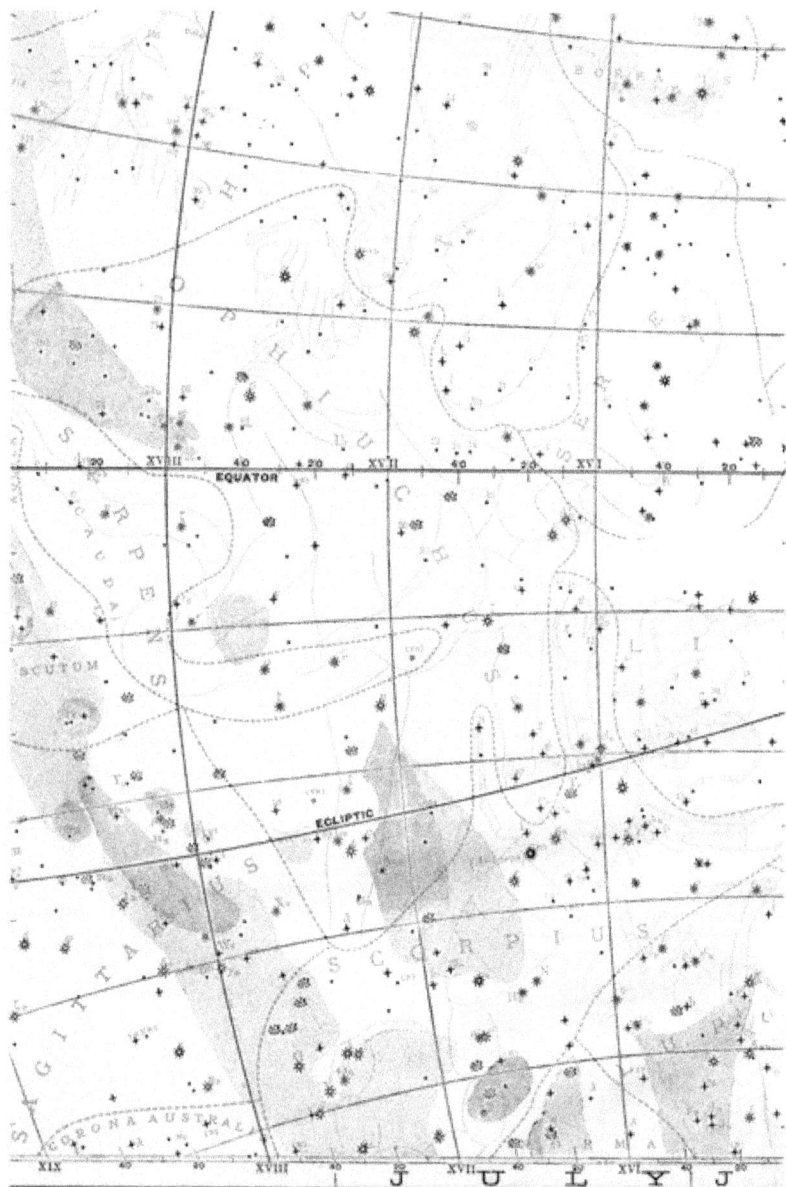

EQUATOR

ECLIPTIC

CORONA AUSTRAL

● *brighter than 1st Mag.* ✹ *1st Mag.* ✷ *2nd Mag.* ✸ *3rd Mag.* ✳ *4th Mag.* + *5th Mag.* · *6th M*

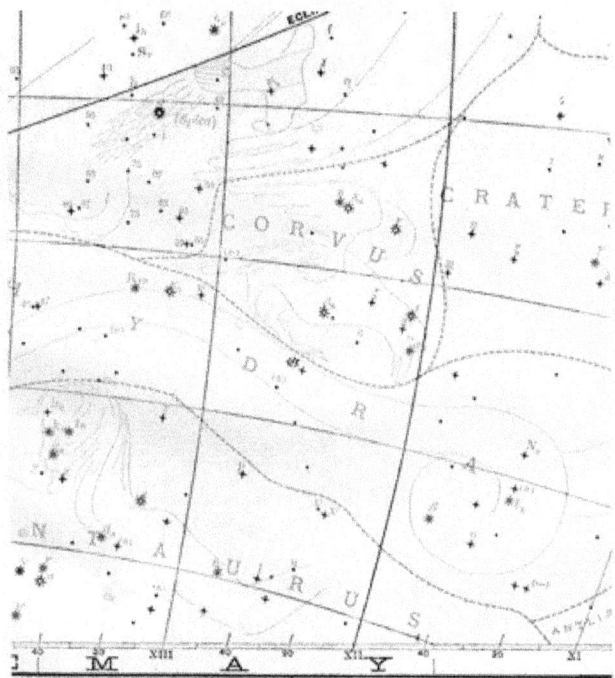

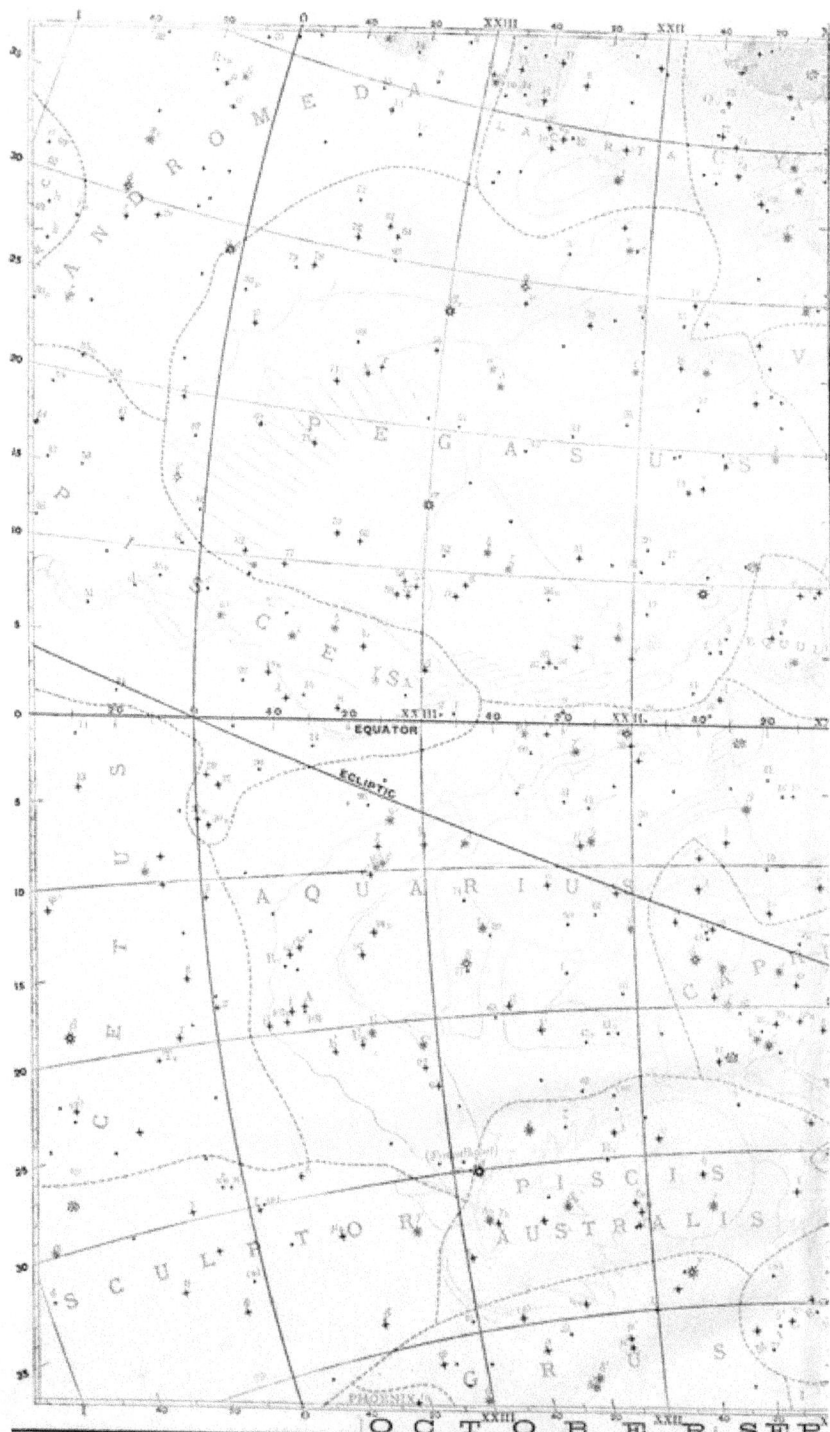

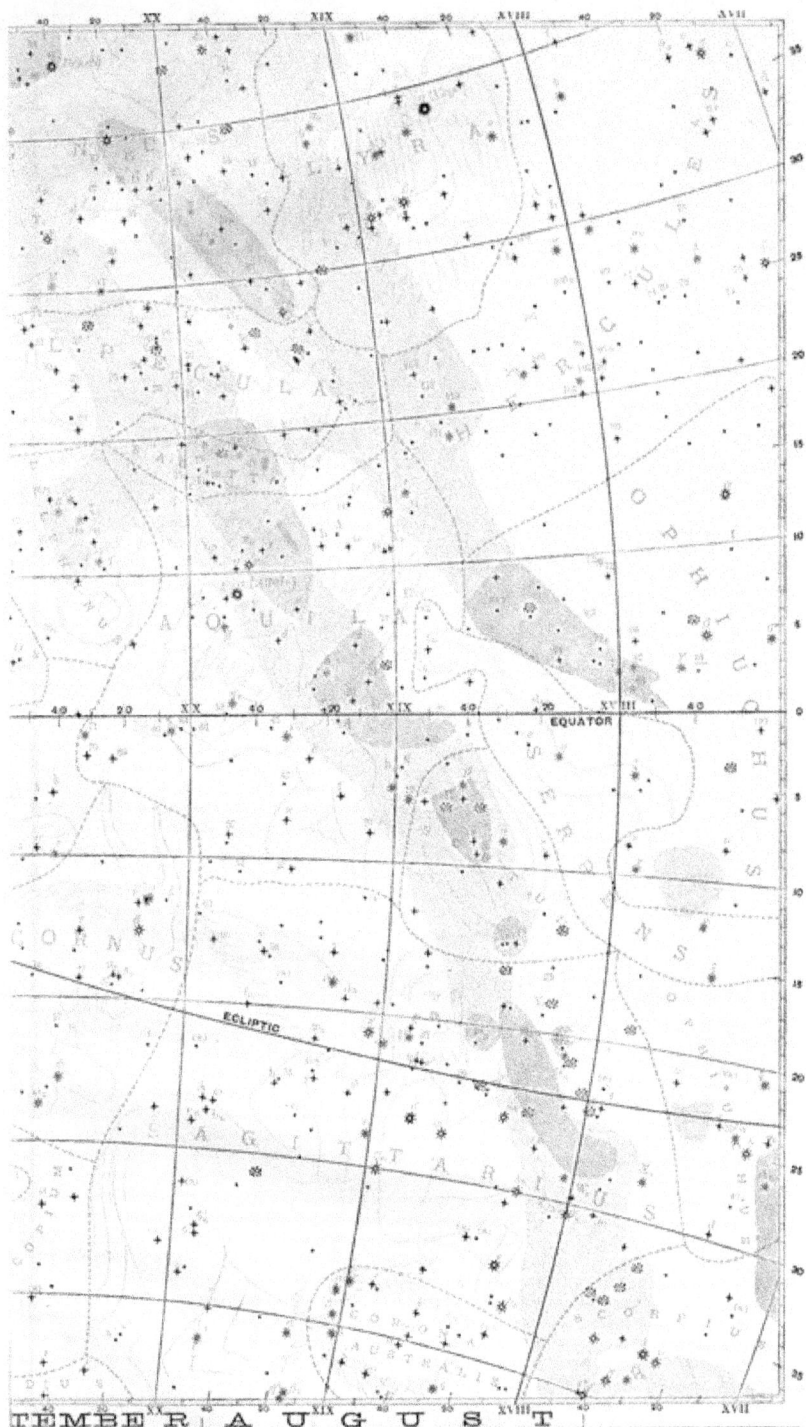

* fainter than 6th Mag.   • red.   ∨ variable.   ∘ double.   — two stars.   ❋ cluster.   ⌣ nebula.

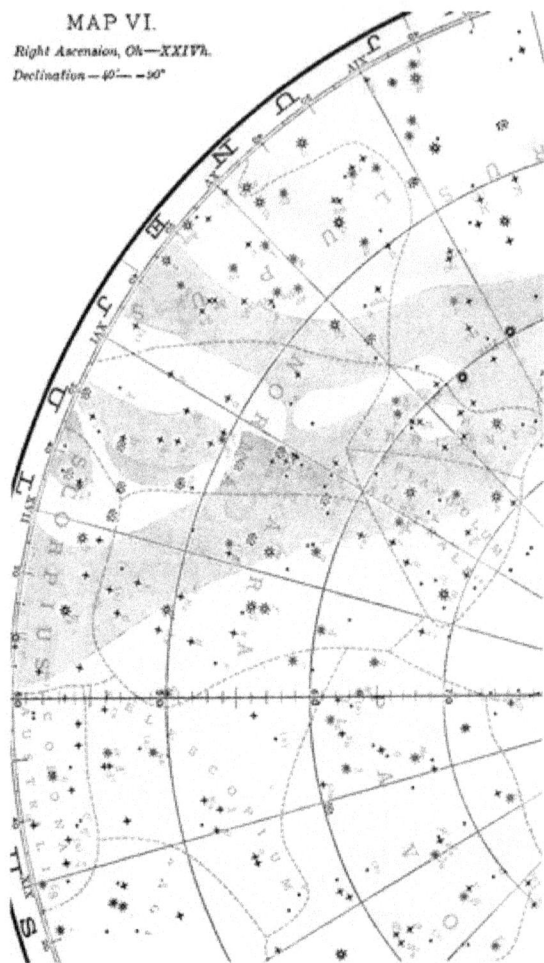

MAP VI.

Right Ascension, 0h — XXIVh.

Declination — 40° — 90°

CONSTELLATIONS
AROUND
SOUTH POLE

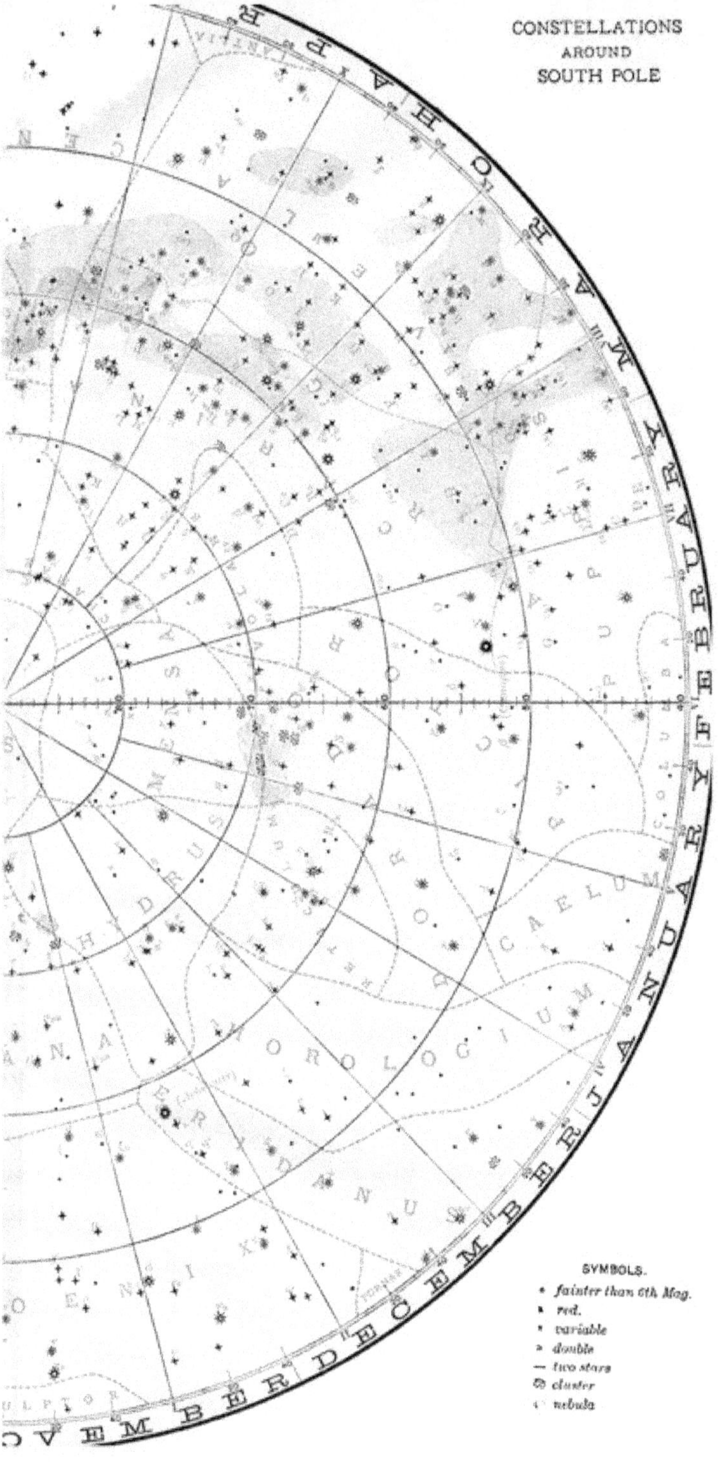

SYMBOLS.
* fainter than 6th Mag.
. red.
* variable
⋗ double
— two stars
⊗ cluster
⊙ nebula

www.ingramcontent.com/pod-product-compliance
Lightning Source LLC
Chambersburg PA
CBHW021633270326
41931CB00008B/995